The Home Meetings

The Unique Way for the Increase and the Building Up of the Church

Witness Lee

Living Stream Ministry
Anaheim, CA • www.lsm.org

First Edition, April 1986.

ISBN 0-87083-231-X

Published by

Living Stream Ministry
2431 W. La Palma Ave., Anaheim, CA 92801 U.S.A.
P. O. Box 2121, Anaheim, CA 92814 U.S.A.

Printed in the United States of America

04 05 06 07 08 09 / 9 8 7 6 5 4 3

CONTENTS

PREFACE

The messages contained in this book concerning the home meetings were given in Anaheim, California in August and September of 1985. They were initially entitled *The Up-to-Date Move of the Lord.*

CHAPTER ONE

THE UNIQUE WAY FOR THE INCREASE AND THE BUILDING UP OF THE CHURCH

Scripture Reading: Acts 2:46-47; 5:42; 6:7; 8:1, 4; 9:31

My burden is to share with you all on a very particular matter. Since the Lord began His recovery among us over sixty years ago, we have been seeking to find out what is the right way and the proper way for the believers in Christ to meet. We were clear that the way Christianity takes to meet together was not according to the Bible and it was not so profitable. Throughout all the years we studied the Bible, and we studied the history of all the different Christian groups, yet we did not know what would be the right way to meet. This question had become more serious year after year. When I went to Taiwan in the fall of 1984, I went through the New Testament thoroughly once more. I know where the verses are concerning this problem, so I put them all together and had a bird's-eye view. I thank the Lord that He has opened up my eyes.

THE UNIQUE WAY TO MEET

When the day of Pentecost came the church began with one hundred twenty as the initiation. Then that initiation brought in on the very first day of the church life three thousand, then on another day five thousand. They began to meet not according to the Jewish congregational way of the Old Testament, nor according to the Roman way, nor according to the Greek way. Then who invented the way for the first group of Christians to meet? The Holy Spirit invented the way. We can say this because on that day, the one hundred twenty were filled with the Holy Spirit economically. And no doubt, the three thousand new converts were also filled with the Holy Spirit. Therefore, whatever they did on that day was initiated by the Holy Spirit. The main thing they did was to begin to meet in the temple for big congregations and in the homes. I like the two phrases in Acts 2:46, "day by day" and "from house to house." It is clear that the way they met had two sides. Perhaps at least three thousand met daily in the temple, a big meeting place. And at the same time they met day by day in the homes.

According to the Greek expression in Acts 2:46 they met from house to house. This indicates that they did not select some houses which would fit their purpose. They met from house to house. They included every house. Today we should have our home meetings entirely according to the Holy Spirit's created and ordained way. According to our feeling we may say, "How could every brother have a meeting in his home? There are so many weaker ones. Oh, we had better consider and select some stronger ones." But we must realize that selecting is not the Holy Spirit's way—it is the human way. In Chinese this phrase means door after door. This indicates no selection, no missing. Whether you are weak or strong, whether old or young, whether knowledgeable or unknowledgeable, as long as you are a believer you meet in your home. Do you dare do this? You say yes in the meeting, but after the meeting, some may say there is no way to practice this. Some would say, "We selected thirty homes, but eventually fifteen have been sifted." If you would select in this way I am afraid that after another period of time only twelve homes would be left which are good for the home meetings. But you have to see that at the very beginning the way created by the Holy Spirit and ordained by God was to meet in two ways, in the congregational way and in the home way, not in selected homes, but in all homes. If you are a Christian, if you are a believer, you have to open up your home for meeting. This is the first pattern at the initiation of the church life.

Since the Lord has shown this, I have begun to see all the benefits of this God-created-and-ordained way. If a new one would believe in the Lord, be baptized, and right away begin to open up his home for meetings, this opening up of his home would encourage him and even uphold him. Therefore, we can see that the home meetings are the top way, the super way, and eventually the unique way to meet.

I fully realize and agree that to have every believer open up his home for meetings is not an easy thing. This is because not everyone would pick up the burden to teach the divine truths or to preach the gospel. Some are not so eloquent and would never speak openly. Others have natural eloquence, but they do not have the spiritual knowledge and do not know the contents of the Bible.

THE WAY OF TODAY'S CHRISTIANITY

The God-ordained way lasted a very short time. Right after the departure of all the apostles, this way began to wane and by the second century, according to my knowledge of church history, was altogether given up. The church by the second century picked up the congregational way according to the worldly way. As a result they needed the big evangelists. They formed monasteries, ancient seminaries, to train people. Today Christianity's existence depends upon the seminaries. Without the seminaries, where could they get preachers? There would be no place to get the people trained to preach or teach. Then all these trained and taught preachers and teachers became the clergy. Then through clergy, hierarchy has been built up. This is today's organized Christianity, and this is the organizational way of today's Christianity. We all hate hierarchy and reject the clergy-laity system. But unconsciously even today to some extent clergy creeps in among us.

I am afraid that even while we have been talking about meeting in the homes we do not have a meeting in every home but rather in a selected way. Some might have said already, "We don't have that many big speakers, do we?" To have a big hall with a big number of people coming together with a big speaker is the Christianity way to worship God today. They do not see how the home meetings are needed. This God-invented way was altogether lost by Christianity.

Zinzendorf, three centuries ago, began to practice the church life. It was quite good in a sense. But Zinzendorf did not say anything about the home meetings. Then after Zinzendorf, one century later, the Brethren were raised up in England. They paid much attention to the way to meet. They wrote books on this. When I was young I was with them for seven and a half years. I never heard the term "home meeting." Every week I attended five meetings among them. All the time I went to that one meeting hall. They only met in that one meeting hall. They never met in any other's home. The Lord in these days has shown us the lack, the loss, and the damage we have been suffering by missing the home meetings. The big speakers with big congregations could only bring in people. There is no way for the big congregations to build up the saints.

BUILDING THE CHURCH THROUGH THE SMALL GROUPS

The way to build the church may be illustrated by the building of this hall. When we built this hall I gave a rough design and the brothers made the drawings. Every day in the early morning, I was watching and observing. One brother was the purchaser. He collected all the materials. Trucks of materials came. If we had only one brother to collect and pile up all the materials on the ground for nine years, they would be ruined. To collect the materials is one thing, but to get all the materials built together is another thing. Look at this building today. In this hall you cannot see one individual piece of material. You can only see one building.

Another brother was directing every group. At that time we had over eighty full-timers whom this brother formed into groups. One group made the stairway, and a group of sisters sanded the handrails on the stairway. They were all grouped together to do a certain part for the building and eventually to put all the pieces together. Now we are enjoying the building.

In the early days of the church life, when the apostles were first raised up by the Lord, they built the church in this way. It was very quick. The church in Jerusalem was built up. Acts 9:31 says, "So the church throughout the whole of Judea and Galilee and Samaria had peace, being built up." In a short time they were all built up. Could we say that all the churches in the U.S.A. have been built up? You cannot say that we have been built up because we have never taken the building way. What is the building way? Small groups! Home meetings!

The big speakers are useful. Peter was useful. Peter spoke to the big congregations and his speaking brought in thousands of people. But that was only one side. There was another side. They met in their homes, in their houses, from house to house. There was no time for them to train preachers. There was no time for them to learn the truth. They had heard only one message and that message was their New Testament. On the day of Pentecost their New Testament was so short, just one message given by Peter in Acts 2. But everybody heard that, everybody learned of that, and everybody spoke that. On the day Peter spoke the message they all got baptized. Then I believe that night they went back home and began to meet, repeating what they had heard from Peter. I believe this shows that everybody can teach and everybody can preach.

If you open up your home for meetings, you will feel there are some things there that need to be cleared up. However, if you do not open up your home, you will leave those things there, maybe for three years. You will come to the big congregations without any feeling about those black, dark things. If you would open up your home, you would consider before you lose your temper with your wife. You would think that after half an hour all the saints will come to meet. This is just something on the negative side, but there are a lot of benefits, a lot of blessings, on the positive side. When saints come into your home they all come in with God; they all come in with Christ; they all come in with a lot of prayer to bless your home. One will step in and say, “Lord, bless this home.” And another one will say, “Bless this family. Lord, remember them all.” The Lord will answer the prayers, and there will be much blessing for you. You may say you are so weak, but if you will open up your home, many will come in who are not so weak. You may be poor, but those who come are rich. The home meeting will rescue you, strengthen you, and enrich you.

THE NATURAL CONCEPT

Christianity's way to meet is according to the natural concept. In human history you could see this kind of congregation. Even the Greek word *ekklesia* was a word for a called out congregation of a city. A call was given that all the city people should come together for a certain purpose, so there was a congregation. Thus, to meet in today's Christianity way, to have the great congregations, is altogether natural, worldly, according to human society. I have never heard of any kind of movement or any kind of culture which invented this way of meeting in every home. Such a thing is only in the Bible. At the very initiation of the church life the saints met from house to house. This is quite extraordinary. This is not following the natural way.

Our problem today is that we were born natural. We were born into the worldly way. Even before we were saved, when we were invited to come to the "church," we would ask who the speaker would be. If we were told Doctor So-and-so would be speaking, then we would come. This is the natural way. Even among us, if the announcement is given that there is to be a meeting next Saturday, many of us would ask who the speaker would be. Who will speak may decide whether or not we will come. This has been wrought into our blood. If we mean business with the Lord to see the real increase of the church and the building up of the church we must repudiate the Christianity way. We must get this blood out of our being. I still treasure the big meetings, but if we have only the big meetings we are like a 747 that has only one wing. How could we fly? We need the two sides. We need the big meetings and the small meetings as well.

You may ask, "Without the big meetings how could we have the increase?" In the sixties when I came to this country, the evangelist Dr. Billy Graham was promoting small group meetings. Because Billy Graham found out that many brought to the gospel were scattered in the denominations and eventually became cold, he encouraged people to form small groups to have Bible study and to pray together. What he promoted was the same in principle as what we are talking about. Although thousands of people may be brought in without the small groups, how many of them could remain? There is no way. It is just like bringing the water out of a deep well and pouring it on the earth. All the water will sink back. We may get the increase, but without the small group meetings they cannot remain in the church to be built up.

Even in Taiwan over a hundred thousand were baptized through our preaching, but I doubt if twenty percent are left. So many were lost because of no home meetings. This is absolutely different from what was practiced in the early days after Pentecost. At Pentecost through the big congregations people were brought in and right away they were put into the home meetings. In the home meetings they were upheld, in the home meetings they were kept, in the home meetings they grew, and in the home meetings they were built up together.

We should not despise the big meetings, but we must match the big meetings with the small groups. We should pay sixty percent of our attention to the small meetings and only forty percent to the big meetings. But I am a little concerned that many pay eighty percent or more of their attention to the big meetings. Many, according to their concept, would say that they prefer to go to the big meetings rather than the home meetings. We need a change of concept! We need both. Without one brother purchasing the materials and collecting them, surely we could not have built this hall. But after the collection of the materials we surely needed another brother to assign all these materials to the builders. In the building of the hall we had a good situation, but today in the building of the church we are short of this. I say this especially to the leading ones of all the churches; what you have been doing is just to maintain a meeting situation of the church. As you do not have small groups, how could you have the building up? It is impossible. I still remember meeting with the Brethren assembly for seven and a half years. Every week I attended five meetings. Yet there was very little contact with any of the others. Of course, we are much better than that. After the meeting we have much contact with each other, but we still do not have much positive building because we are short of the home meetings. We must see the need of the home meetings. Without home meetings there can be no building.

THE KNOWLEDGE OF THE TRUTH AND THE GROWTH IN LIFE FOR THE HOME MEETINGS

In the coming messages, my burden is to share with you how to have the home meetings, how to make them rich, strong, fresh, living, so attractive, even so attracting, and able to uphold people.

Many of us are very much concerned for the home meetings because it is not so easy for the home meetings to be rich, strong, fresh, living, attractive, and able to uphold people. In the big meetings we only need two or three trained and selected ones. If you have a Billy Graham you can hold thousands of people. You may argue that you do not have such a one in your home meeting. But praise the Lord, we have thousands of small potatoes. All these have to be made useful.

How do you have a meeting in your home which is rich, strong, fresh, living, attractive, and able to uphold? Acts 5:42 says, "And every day, in the temple and from house to house, they did not cease teaching and bringing the good news of Jesus as the Christ." The word teaching means they knew the truth. And bringing the good news of Jesus as the Christ means they were preaching. They were able to teach, and they were able to preach. In the past we have had conferences and annual trainings, both summer and winter. We have finished the entire study of the whole New Testament, and the messages have been printed. Many of you have the complete set of life-studies of the New Testament in your home on the shelves. Yet how much of the truth conveyed in those pages of the life-studies has really gotten into you? And how many truths are you able to teach others? I am a little concerned that it is not too many.

We have also stressed the growth in life very much. We need to know the truth and we need to grow in life. Yet again, how much growth have you had in the past years? According to my observation, it is not too much. In one sense, it is disappointing. Yet in another sense, it is encouraging because you are still here. You are still seeking, hungry, and thirsty.

I realize we have put out the truths, but we have helped the saints grow in life in a very loose way. In a sense, I regret, but I must tell you, I had no choice in the past, even in the coming days I still have no choice. I must spend the time to put out the Word of God. Brother Nee, like others who have gone before us, knew so much, yet not very much of what he knew is left. We only have some of the books. From this I realized that I must take the time to put out whatever the Lord has shown us in these years and get it into print.

I believe there will be a period of time for the Lord to do something to build up His church before He comes back. Because of this I anticipate a great need for the life-studies in the future. I am still burdened to put out the life-studies on the Pentateuch and the prophets of the Old Testament. I must spend at least half of my time to get these things written, spoken, and published. Then I still have the burden to take care of a few regions, for example, Taiwan. There is the need to go back again and again. I am also endeavoring to do more than what I did in the past for the churches in the U.S. From now on I would like to have more time with you and with the leading ones, charging all of us to be definite. Although we have life-studies on the twenty-seven books of the New Testament, the saints must get into them. We must get into what is taught in Matthew, what is taught in Mark, what is taught in Luke, what is taught in John, in Acts, and so forth. This needs some time.

The educational system in the human race has been practiced for thousands of years. Now the entire world follows the same kind of educational system. You have kindergarten, elementary, junior high, high school, then college and graduate school. If you teach people in mathematics in a loose way without following this educational system, when they become old, they will not know much. You must have a definite way to charge people to finish the course. Six years are required to finish elementary school, another six years to finish high school, then another four years to finish college. After they have finished this they will have received definite training. We must follow this way. So we all have to endeavor. By the small groups we have the way to do this. Suppose a school with a thousand students has no classes formed but only invites people to give good speeches all year round. The students will get something, but only in a very loose and general way. But if I were to open a school, I would not invite good speakers but rather good teachers. I would build up classrooms, form the classes, and put in the best teachers. Then they would teach the classes semester after semester. I would not need to invite a good speaker. I would have a strong school built up and all the students who graduate from my school would be very definitely educated. We must learn this way. Our classes are the small groups. We must form the small groups.

At one time in Dallas there were two particular Baptist congregations. One depended upon having a good speaker for the big congregation, while the other one depended upon classes. After some years the one which was for the big meetings, which had the big number, eventually came to a failure with a small number. But the one which paid attention to classes and which had a small number at the beginning, eventually had a number about ten times more than the other one.

Just to have general conferences to give certain messages does not work too well. We need to set up classrooms with definite teachers. But where are our classrooms? Every home is a classroom. And every brother or sister of that certain home should be the teacher. You have to set up your home as a classroom. Get yourself educated and trained as a teacher. Then along with this, a good teacher must be a grown-up person. Although a child may have the best knowledge, he could not be a good teacher. Therefore we need to grow in life. All the churches have to endeavor to educate every saint fully in the spiritual truths, and to cause them all to grow in life. Only these two things could qualify all the saints to be good for the home meetings.

We have to believe that in a home meeting of five or six at least two or three could be and should be rich in the knowledge of the truth, and rich in the growth of life. When they come together these two or three will spontaneously become the richness, the strength, the newness, the livingness, the attracting power, and the upholding power of that small group. They could be useful and their usefulness could be applied to the practical situation. However, listening to a speaker in a large congregation, in a sense, annuls their usefulness. So from now on I would advise all the churches to only have at most one big meeting every week. Do not treasure Brother Lee's speaking; you all have to come together to practice speaking. Do not say you do not know how. Just speak. Every one of you can be an apostle, an evangelist, a teacher, and a shepherd.

I hope that you would be deeply impressed to repudiate the over-treasuring of the congregational way and to realize the need for the small groups. Then secondly, I hope that you would be deeply impressed to pick up the adequate knowledge of the truth. Try to study the New Testament and try to spend time to get into the life-studies. I like to see saints' homes where there are life-studies in every room so that anytime, anywhere, they can get into them. But I am afraid that in your home all the life-studies are piled up on the shelves. Get into the full knowledge of the truth and then pray to the Lord, "Lord grant me mercy and grace that I would grow in You. Grace me to grow, Lord." Pray much, seeking the growth in life. You will be enlivened. You will be a factor to enrich, to strengthen, to refresh, and to enliven the home meetings. Then the home meetings will be attractive and will be able to uphold any member.

CHAPTER TWO

THE WAY TO BE EQUIPPED FOR THE HOME MEETINGS

(1)

Scripture Reading: Eph. 5:18-20; Acts 13:52; 2:46; Rom. 14:17; Eph. 3:14, 16-19

MEETING IN EVERY HOME

According to our study, experience, and observation, I would say that we have found that the home meetings are the unique way for the increase and building up of the church. There are many positive things that come out of the home meetings. In the home meetings, everyone becomes a seeking one, a serving one, a preaching one, a teaching one, and one that spontaneously witnesses for the Lord. We hope to encourage all the saints in the Lord's recovery to have meetings in their homes.

The Greek phrase in Acts 5:42 indicates that not one house was missed. They met from house to house. We should not take the way of selecting some promising homes, and then having the meetings in those promising homes. This is wrong. Every home of the believers is promising. We need to open up our home. First we can meet with our folks. We do not need to meet with others first. We can initiate our home meeting by meeting with our family members. We who have wives and children all can have a home meeting. We just meet with our folks, with our wife, and with our little children. To set up a meeting will stir up our heart and will fan the flame in our heart and in our spirit. First of all, we will be burned, and then our family will be burned. To set up a home meeting will keep out many evil things from our homes.

Do not say that you are weak, that you cannot overcome your self, that you cannot overcome your temper, that you cannot control yourself, that you cannot do this or that. Just set up a home meeting in your home. I have seen in many cases that when you set up a meeting in your home the Holy Spirit brings people to you. Gradually people will come. I would say that if you are a Christian, yet you do not have a home meeting, you are not up to the standard. You may know the Bible, be spiritual, be seeking, love the Lord, and so forth, but if you do not open your home, you are not up to the standard. Even a single sister could open her apartment for meetings. Every lodging of the saints, whether single or with a family, should be opened up for meeting. You may say, "With whom do we meet?" First, with the angels, then with a believer, then with a neighbor. You must pray, endeavor, and even fast until you get a neighbor to come to meet with you. If you determine to have some meeting with you in your home, surely there is a way. A lot of persons are around you every day. You have a lot of relatives and friends.

Are you going to be holy? Set up a home meeting. Are you going to be spiritual? Set up a home meeting. Are you going to know the Bible? Nothing will force you to seek the knowledge of the Bible more than setting up a home meeting. The home meetings will force you to seek after the proper, spiritual knowledge, and while you are seeking the knowledge for teaching others, you yourself will be taught, enlightened, and nourished. I can recall my own history. When I was trying to teach others I began to realize that I needed to be taught. The definite, single, and sole step for the Lord's recovery to take today is to promote the home meetings. This is the unique way.

THE CHRISTIAN MEETING BEING A MATTER OF OUR SPIRIT

In one sense, for everyone to come together to have home meetings is an easy thing, but in another sense, it is the hardest thing. The most difficult thing is to have the home meetings. Why? Because for Christians to gather together is not a natural thing. It should not be done in a natural way but rather in the spiritual way. So, we studied much concerning this matter, and thus far, we are still not so sure what is the best way to build up the home meetings. We are trying our best to read, to study, to check out, and even to examine and determine the best way to have the home meetings. Thus far, I can tell you that to have the home meetings depends altogether upon our spirit.

Those who are too much for the Pentecostal movement would say, "Well, if you don't have the Holy Ghost, you just cannot have any kind of meeting. A Christian meeting depends upon the Holy Ghost." But I was in such meetings for some time and I did not see that those meetings were so good in the most proper way. After reading the Scriptures again and again and checking with our experiences, we realized that for Christians to meet is altogether a matter of our spirit.

If you are going to play a certain sport you have to use the right members of your body. To use your ears, nose, lips, or teeth to play football would be nonsensical. You may say that you depend upon the Holy Ghost, but to depend upon the Holy Ghost you need the proper organ. You cannot depend upon the Holy Ghost by your mind; the mind is not the right organ to touch the Holy Spirit. There is only one organ created by God for you to touch the Holy Spirit—your human spirit. Romans 8:16 says, "The Spirit Himself witnesses with our spirit." It is the Spirit with your spirit. The Spirit works, yet He works by a certain organ.

For example, all the appliances in this building are operated by electricity. But electricity only operates by a definite means, that is, by the wire and the switch. If you do not install wire into this building with a switch, the electricity will not work. The problem today is not with the Holy Spirit, because according to the entire New Testament revelation the Holy Spirit has been given and has also been poured out. The Holy Spirit today is the very consummation of the Triune God. He has gone through incarnation, human living, crucifixion, and resurrection. Now He is the life-giving Spirit as the consummation of the Triune God. In John 16:15 the Lord Jesus tells us that all that the Father has has been given to Him. Now all that He is and has is fully realized in the Spirit. Hence, the Spirit is the consummation of the Triune God, and this consummated Holy Spirit is ready. Today in the whole universe this consummated Holy Spirit is ready for God's seekers to open up and receive Him. By what organ do we receive Him? By our spirit!

Today, when we preach the gospel to sinners, mainly we have to approach their conscience. If we only teach their mind to know God, to understand the Bible, and to understand the gospel, that is not adequate. The best and most effective way to preach the gospel is to touch a sinner's conscience, for the conscience is the main part of the human spirit. When we touch a person's conscience, we touch their spirit. This is why when we preach the gospel, we must do it with the convicting power to convince them and to convict them in their conscience. Then, when their conscience is touched, they begin to repent, to weep, and sometimes even to cry. We cannot teach people's minds to weep; we have to touch their conscience. The conscience is the main working part of our human spirit, and when we exercise our conscience, we exercise our spirit. When we pray, and repent, and speak to the Lord, we exercise our spirit. When we do this, right away the Holy Spirit gets into us. This is the only way for us to touch the Holy Spirit, the consummated Spirit as the very consummation of the Triune God. But this principle has been very much neglected, and even missed by today's Christians.

Some think that the best way to get the Spirit is to pray and pray. That is right. The best way to touch the Spirit is to pray, but you have to pray with a right understanding. The ones in the Pentecostal movement always teach people that they have to fast, to pray, and to wait on God until suddenly something happens to them. Then you get the Holy Ghost. They say that the best way to receive the Holy Ghost is to turn your jaw and turn your tongue to utter something in a strange voice, that is, to speak in tongues. I tried many different ways, but I must tell you that the biblical way is to pray in your spirit. You do not need to wait, and you do not need to turn your jaw, and you do not need to turn your tongue; you just need to pray from within your spirit. If you will do this for just a minute, you will touch the Holy Spirit.

Today, to touch the electricity in this building is easy; just go to the switch. Suppose you kneel down, begging and praying, "Dear electricity, please come to me. I'm waiting on you. Don't you know this? Answer me. Please come!" If the electricity could speak, it would say, "Stupid guy, why don't you touch the switch?" Every morning you have to pray, not just to ask the Lord to give you a good day, but to open yourself up again in your spirit. Open up your spirit to the Lord, "Lord, thank You." Sometimes you only need to say, "Lord, thank You. Thank You that I can contact You here." You can say, "Lord, thank You. Thank You that Your blood cleanses me. Thank You, Lord, that You are with me." When you do this, you have the sense that deep within you, that is, in your spirit, you are touching the Lord, you are touching the Spirit. We all know this, but too many times we pray so many things which distract us from touching the Spirit.

TO BE FILLED IN OUR SPIRIT

The Christian meeting is altogether a matter of our spirit. Concerning this, there are two very strategic points. First, if you are going to get yourself equipped so that you may be used by the Lord to bless the home meetings, you have to be filled in your spirit. Ephesians 5 shows us such an excellent revelation concerning God's economy of Christ and the church. It seems strange that all of a sudden it says, "And do not be drunk with wine" (Eph. 5:18). We know that to be drunk with wine is to be filled in our body with the physical wine. Do not go that way, but be filled, not in your body nor in your mind, but in your spirit. Be filled in *your* spirit. The King James and some other versions render this verse wrongly. Their translators thought that the spirit here refers to the Holy Spirit. According to the context, if you read the entire chapter, you can see that the spirit here does not refer to the Holy Spirit. It refers rather to your regenerated spirit, which is indwelt by the Holy Spirit. As a seeking Christian you should not be filled in your body with some physical thing; you should be filled in your spirit.

God made our spirit in a unique way, so that it could never be invaded by anything other than God. The Bible implies that God created one organ in our being to be the very central organ, that is our human spirit. This is an extraordinary organ in our human being. It is hard to find a verse indicating that our human spirit could be occupied by anything other than God. Even the unbelievers' spirit is kept by God purposely for Himself.

This is why Ephesians 5:18 says to be filled in this organ. Be filled in your spirit with what? Ephesians does not say, nor does it need to say. When it says, "Be filled in spirit," surely it means be filled in your spirit with God. How can we know this? To know the Bible is not by our imagination, but always by its context. I do not think many among us have ever paid adequate attention to the context of Ephesians 5:18. Verse 13 says, "But all things which are exposed are made manifest by the light; for everything that makes manifest is light." This word brings us into light. Then it continues from verse 14: "Wherefore He says, Awake, sleeper, and arise from among the dead, and Christ shall shine on you. Look therefore carefully how you walk, not as unwise, but as wise, redeeming the time, because the days are evil. Therefore do not be foolish, but understand what the will of the Lord is. And...." "And" here means after all this, in addition to all this you add something: "Do not be drunk with wine, in which is dissipation, but be filled in spirit." The next verse says, "Speaking to one another." Right after "be filled in spirit" you have the word "speaking." This kind of phrase could be considered as a modifier. "Speaking to one another" modifies "be filled." How could you be filled? It is by speaking. By speaking, you will be filled in your spirit. But is it by speaking to one another in murmuring or gossip? Should we speak to one another about the world news, America today, school, family, computers? What should we speak in? We should speak in psalms, such as Psalm 119, a long piece which has 176 verses of 22 sections according to the Hebrew alphabet.

Verses 19 and 20 say, "Speaking to one another in psalms

and hymns and spiritual songs, singing and psalming with your heart to the Lord, giving thanks at all times for all things." Four things are mentioned here: speaking, singing, psalming with your heart to the Lord, and giving thanks at all times for all things. Give thanks not only at the time you gain some profit, but also at the time when you suffer a loss; not only at the time when your wife gives you a happy face, but also when she gives you a long face. When she drops her face you have to say, "Lord, thank You" even the more. When you have a car accident you have to say, "Thank You, Lord." You have to give thanks at all times for all things bad or good.

In these verses there are four modifiers: speaking, singing, psalming, and giving thanks. All these modify "be filled." Strictly speaking, I am not a light person who is easily excited, so it is hard for me to be rejoicing or to be joyful. But a number of times when I read a hymn and spoke the hymn to another person, I got excited. For instance, you just speak that hymn, "Oh, what a life! Oh, what a peace!" You may think that this has nothing to do with the meeting, but speaking to one another indicates a kind of meeting. If you speak to your wife that means you are meeting with your wife. That is the initiation or start of your home meeting. Speaking to one another indicates a kind of meeting. In today's Christianity have you ever found a place where people meet together to speak the hymns? It is easy for people to sing the hymns, but not to speak the hymns. We have to practice this. Speaking the hymns is not my invention. This is clearly mentioned here by Paul: "Be filled in spirit, speaking to one another in psalms and hymns and spiritual songs, singing and psalming with your heart to the Lord." However, we are not used to doing this.

Now we are going to have home meetings. We all know the problem. Suppose six to eight of us come together. You look at me, and I nod to you. We just do not know what to do. First, we Christians should be people who are all the time filled in our spirit, not just at the time of worship, not just at the time of prayer, not just at the time of morning watch, nor just at the time of the meeting. All the time we must be persons filled in our spirit. We must practice this. Do not practice this just whenever you come to the small meeting. Practice this in your home, in your daily life, from morning to evening. Practice being filled in your spirit with God, with Christ, with the Spirit, with all His praises. The best way to help us do this is to speak the hymns. If you do not have any persons to speak to, you had better speak to the air, to the window, toward the lawn, the trees, the flowers, and sometimes to the cats, dogs, or birds. Speak to your wife and let your wife speak to you. Do not speak ordinary words; speak psalms and hymns. Hymn #501 is a good hymn for speaking. "O glorious Christ, Savior mine, Thou art truly radiance divine." Speak to one another. Practice this and you will be equipped for the home meeting. Then when you come in, you need not wait, and you need not look at others. You just say, "Brothers, may we speak a hymn?" Sometimes if you ask to sing a hymn, the answer may be that no one knows the melody and that no one can lead the singing. But everybody can speak. Yet to speak from the spirit requires exercise. You need to exercise to speak, to speak with your spirit.

Ephesians 5:18b says, "Be filled in spirit," and 19a says, "Speaking to one another in psalms and hymns and spiritual songs." I believe this could be done mainly in the home meetings. It is hard for us to do this in a big meeting, but it is very good to do this with five, six, seven, or eight. When six or eight come together, one says, "Brothers, let us speak Hymn #501." You speak from the spirit and the others follow in the spirit. If you speak from your natural voice, the others would follow in the same way. If you open in the right way to speak, "Oh, what a life! Oh, what a peace!" *(Hymns,* #499), others will follow. Right away the meeting begins in a living way. This kind of speaking inspires people, stirs people up, and quite often nourishes people.

The Recovery Version translates Acts 13:52 as follows: "The disciples were made full of joy and of the Holy Spirit." Actually, "made full" in the Greek text is just one word, "filled." The disciples were filled with joy and with the Holy Spirit. The verse is translated in this way because Acts uses two words for filling and it is hard to find equivalents for these two words in the English language. One is *pletho,* to fill outwardly; the other is *pleroo,* to fill inwardly. On the day of Pentecost the Holy Spirit came down upon the disciples, and they were filled outwardly *(pletho,* Acts 2:4). At the same time the wind filled the house inwardly *(pleroo,* Acts 2:2). The second word, *pleroo,* is used again in Acts 13:52. The disciples were filled within. This verse says that they were filled with joy and with the Holy Spirit. Whenever you are filled within with the Spirit, you are also full of joy. This is why the kingdom of God, the church life in Romans 14, is "righteousness and peace and joy in the Holy Spirit" (v. 17). You have to exercise righteousness for yourself, and you have to exercise peace with others. Then you must have joy in the Holy Spirit with God all the time. You must be a joyful person. You must be a person of joy. You could only be this kind of person by being filled with the Holy Spirit. This is not the tongue-speaking; this is not the outpouring of the Spirit upon you. This is the infilling, the inward filling of the Holy Spirit within you.

In Acts 13:52 the believers were filled with joy and with the Holy Spirit. I do believe this was not only in their daily life. At that time their meeting life was a great part of their daily life, because every day they met from house to house. They were joyful people. In Acts 2:46 they broke bread from house to house and they ate food with exultation. Exultation is rejoicing, a crazy joy, a kind of ecstasy. You are so happy, so joyful, that you are crazy; you are a drunkard. That was the way they met in the homes, and that attracted people. Those whom the Lord added were attracted by their exultation.

Suppose you had six brothers and sisters meeting together and you brought in two or three new ones. If all six of you were so sad, not doing anything, but just expressing yourselves in this way, every new one would go away. The husband would say, "We have tasted this kind of atmosphere enough already. In my home I saw my wife's face like this." Or the wife would say, "In my home I saw my husband's long face for quite a long time. I don't like to see this kind of face anymore. I don't like to taste this." But suppose all six of the brothers and sisters were excited, not performing, but filled with joy, eating food with exultation. Every new one would be inspired and attracted. In Acts this eating food with exultation was related to the home meetings. Every day the believers broke bread from house to house and they ate food with exultation, praising God.

If your spirit is not filled with the Holy Spirit, how could you be joyful? How could you be exultant? So we all have to see this. We need to be filled with the Holy Spirit all the time, every day. When we come together, the only way that could help us to be so full of the Holy Spirit is to speak, first to speak a psalm, to speak a hymn, and even to speak a song. Then we sing the short pieces and psalm the long pieces. We all need to practice this. Then we will be persons equipped for the home meetings.

TO BE STRENGTHENED INTO THE INNER MAN

Second, to be equipped for the home meetings, we must be strengthened into our inner man. Paul prayed for this in Ephesians 3:14-19. Bowing his knees unto the Father, he prayed that the Father would grant the believers to be strengthened into the inner man. Paul uses several phrases to modify this strengthening. He prayed that the Father would grant you to be strengthened according to the riches of His glory, with power, and through His Spirit. God would strengthen you according to the riches of His glory. It is not a small thing for God to do this. God would strengthen you into the inner man, not according to the scarcity of His strength, but according to the riches of His glory with power through the Holy Spirit.

Let me illustrate in this way. Suppose a working brother works the whole day in the office under a lot of pressure and returns home fully exhausted. At home he is offended by some member of his family, perhaps his wife or his mother-in-law. Regardless of how tired he is, he will be so strong in losing his temper. Before this, if you were to ask him to read a page of a life-study, he would say, "No, I can't do it. I'm tired out." Then you may say, "Okay, let us pray about it." But he would reply, "No, I can't do it. I can't. I am dying." But when his mother-in-law provoked him, he got strengthened into his temper with the riches of the Devil's subtlety. His entire being enters into his temper. When you come back home from your tiring job you must pray, "Father, grant me according to the riches of Your glory, with power, through Your Spirit to be strengthened into my inner man." Then your entire being will be concentrated into the inner man, which is your human spirit. Here you can be fully strengthened, you can pray, and you can come to the meeting.

I believe quite often when the saints come to the home meeting, a number of them are tired, especially in the evening. That is the right time for you to be strengthened into the inner man. Do not remain in your tired, worn out body. Do not remain in your mind. Do not remain in your soul. You should pray, "Lord, strengthen me into my spirit." Then by being strengthened into your spirit, you can overcome the tiredness of your body and the tedious feeling in your soul. In the following verses we see that our being strengthened relates to the meeting life. After being strengthened into our inner man, verses 17-19 continue, "That Christ may make His home in your hearts through faith, that you, having been rooted and grounded in love, may be strong to apprehend with all the saints what is the breadth and length and height and depth, and to know the knowledge-surpassing love of Christ, that you may be filled unto all the fullness of God." "With all the saints" indicates some kind of meeting. To be strengthened that you may be strong to apprehend the measurement, the dimensions of Christ with all the saints indicates meeting. Even the "fullness of God" here means the church life, the expression of God. I believe this is related to the meeting.

We all need these two things: to be filled in our spirit with the Holy Spirit and to be strengthened into our spirit. Then we will come to the meeting with our spirit filled just like the four tires on a car. Too many times when we come to the meeting, we come flat. We need to come to the meeting full of air, filled with air, full of the "pum, pum, pum." Even though we may be tired and even worn out by the day, we must be strong in our spirit.

This is not a matter of doctrine. What is needed is much practice. We all need to practice the filling of our spirit and the strengthening of our spirit. We need to practice this if we mean business with the Lord for His recovery. We need this. If we would neglect the home meetings and only care for the big meetings, we would not need much practice. One or two leading ones would do everything for us. They would become the clergy and everyone else would become laymen. That is not the church life. There would be no way for the Lord to build up His Body. The building up all depends upon the home meetings. So all of us have to practice the filling of our spirit and the strengthening into our inner man. Then we will be full of the Triune God, full of His attributes, and we will be strengthened in our spirit. Then when we come together, everyone will be equipped to carry the home meeting on. This is the way. I hope that this would not be just a message to you, but rather a kind of instruction that you would practice. Practice daily to be filled in your spirit and to be strengthened into your inner man.

Chapter Three

THE WAY TO BE EQUIPPED FOR THE HOME MEETINGS

(2)

Scripture Reading: Eph. 3:8; Acts 5:42; 1 Cor. 6:17; 2 Cor. 1:21

In the last message we saw that the way to be equipped for the home meetings is to be filled in spirit and to be strengthened into the inner man. In this message we shall consider two more aspects of the way to be equipped: to experience the unsearchable riches of Christ and to preach Christ as the good news. Surely we need the strengthening. We need the filling. Yet if we have only the filling and the strengthening, we would still not be rich for the home meetings. To be filled is one thing and to be strengthened is another thing. Yet these two could not be our riches. Our riches are just Christ Himself. Therefore, for us to be rich in the home meetings, to have something to minister to other people, we need the experience of the unsearchable riches of Christ.

TO EXPERIENCE THE UNSEARCHABLE RICHES OF CHRIST

Ephesians is a profound book. In chapter three Paul first speaks of the unsearchable riches of Christ (v. 8). Then he goes on to pray that we may be able to comprehend or apprehend with the saints the dimensions of Christ (v. 18). This is to know the breadth, the length, the height, and the depth of the universe. These four dimensions are an illustration of Christ's unlimitedness. What is the height of the universe?

How high is the height? No one can measure it. How long is the universe? Can you measure the length? How broad is the breadth, and how deep is the depth? No one can measure this. These dimensions are used by Paul to speak of the unlimitedness of Christ. Christ is not only rich in what He is, He is also immeasurable in His dimensions. This is marvelous. Whenever I come to such a point, I am in trembling that I may miss the mark due to the shortness of human language, the lack of the adequate expression to tell others what the riches of Christ are. By the Lord's mercy I began to see this about forty years ago. But whenever I spoke on the unsearchable riches of Christ, I regretted that I was so short in the human utterance. In my speaking I was not so adequate to itemize all the riches of Christ.

Our hymnal includes over eight hundred pieces collected from more than ten thousand pieces from different sources. After collecting these top Christian songs, we felt there was a big shortage of hymns on the things that the Lord has shown us in this half century and on the things we have experienced. Hymn #542 was written at the time we were preparing the hymnal. The chorus says:

> O the riches, O the riches,
> Christ my Savior has for me!
> How unsearchable their measure,
> Yet my full reality!

In writing verse 2, I tried to itemize some of the riches: "life and light, wisdom, power, healing, comfort, treasures rich of God's delight." Then verse 3 says:

> God's redemption, full salvation,
> And His resurrection pow'r,
> Sanctifying, glorifying,
> All transcending every hour!

Verse 4 says:

> O the riches of my Savior—
> Nothing less than God as all!

It is easy to say, "Nothing less than God as all," but what is the "all"? Verse 4 continues:

All His person and possessions,
  Now my spirit doth enthrall.

Still, not many riches are itemized. Verses 5 and 6 continue:

O the riches of my Savior!
  Who can know their breadth and length,
Or their depth and height unmeasured,
  Yet they are my joy and strength.

May I know these boundless riches,
  Christ experience in full;

There still is not the adequate itemizing of the riches of Christ.

In the training outlines on *The Conclusion of the New Testament* there is one section on the attributes of Christ in which I counted altogether twenty-two items. But it is not too much to say that there should be two thousand items.

Seeing the Unsearchable Riches of Christ

I would like to impress you that Paul in Ephesians 3:8 says that the "unsearchable riches of Christ" have been shown to him. This verse begins with the phrase, "to me." When I was young and read this, I would say, "I am not that 'me.' That is Paul. He is too great. 'To him' is okay but not 'to me.'" But Paul says "to me." This "me" is "less than the least of all the saints." He was the "leastest," yet this grace was given to him to preach the unsearchable riches of Christ as the gospel.

Preaching the Unsearchable Riches of Christ

Actually, you have to realize that "to preach as the gospel" in Greek is just one word. This word is not the ordinary word in Greek for preach. This is the word that means to preach something as the gospel, to preach something as the glad tidings or as the good news. Therefore, to Paul, his gospel is the all-inclusive Christ. In other words, his gospel is the unsearchable riches of Christ. In this sense the entire book of Ephesians is a gospel because the contents of the gospel preached by Paul are the unsearchable riches of Christ. His gospel is not just about sin. It is not just about going to hell. It is not just about repenting and believing for the forgiveness of sins that you may be reconciled to God, saved from eternal perdition, and have the eternal life. Even if you include eternal life in the contents of the gospel, still that does not compare with what Paul preached. He preached the unsearchable riches of Christ as the gospel.

The Riches of Christ Producing the Fullness

In Ephesians Paul not only refers to the riches of Christ but also to the fullness of Him that fills all in all (1:23). What are the riches? And what is the fullness? The fullness is the issue of the enjoyment of the riches. The riches of Christ are the items of what He is, of what He has, of what He can do, and of what He is doing. But the fullness of Christ is the church produced by the believers' enjoyment of the riches of Christ. We have illustrated this by the situation in America. In the supermarket we have the riches of the U.S.A. But a husky American is the fullness of the enjoyment of all the riches of the U.S.A. The riches of America are here, yet if we do not enjoy them, there will be no fullness of America. There will only be the riches. Some of the young people from the churches in Taiwan and Hong Kong were so short and skinny. But since they came to America, the riches of America have been digested and assimilated into their blood, becoming the tissues and elements of their being. Today, even though they are Chinese, they are the fullness of America. Today we Christians spiritually speaking are so skinny. We do not have the adequate weight. Why are the Christian meetings, whether big or small, mostly very skinny, very poor? Although Christians love the Lord and love to meet together, they have nothing to minister. We are so skinny in the meetings because we do not enjoy the riches of Christ. We do not experience the riches of Christ.

Who Christ Is and Where He Is

To enjoy, that is, to experience the riches of Christ, we have to realize who Christ is today, and where He is. This is something very practical in our daily life. Second Corinthians 1:21

says, “But He who firmly attaches us with you unto Christ and has anointed us is God.” Christ here in Greek means the anointed One. “Attaches us with you unto Christ” is connected with “anointed us.” You cannot separate these two things. The attaching actually is the anointing. God has attached us to Christ, and Christ means the anointed One. God has attached us to the anointed One. Psalm 133 says that the ointment upon the head of Aaron flowed down his beard, and even to the skirts of his long robe. The high priest, Aaron, was God’s anointed, full of the ointment. If you were to become attached to him, you would likewise become anointed. When we paint a house, we say that there is wet paint. If you attach yourself to the freshly painted wall you get painted. In the same way God has attached us to the anointed One, so spontaneously God has anointed us. Christ today possesses the ointment, the paint, with which God has painted us.

God has attached us unto the Anointed. Christ today is the very Anointed. This involves His location. Where is Christ today? To say that Christ is in our spirit may be too doctrinal. The entire New Testament shows us that economically our Christ today is in the heavens. Essentially He is in us. Romans 8:34 says that Christ is at the right hand of God. Yet in the same chapter verse 10 says that Christ is in you. Are these two Christs, one who is in the heavens, and one who is on the earth? Today the Christian teachings are too objective. Christians know that today our Lord is in the third heavens and they are waiting for Him to come back. Yet we have to know that the New Testament also tells us that this heavenly Christ is the Christ in resurrection. This Christ in resurrection is in us essentially. Let me use electricity as an illustration. In our meeting hall there is one electricity. Yet this one electricity is both here in this hall and there in the power plant many miles away. Even before my sentence has been finished, the current of electricity has already traveled between the two places. These are not two electricities but just one. Today the one Christ is both in the heavens and in us.

God has attached us to this anointed Christ who is right now in us. First Corinthians 6:17 is even stronger than this. It says, "He who is joined to the Lord is one spirit." Young sisters, do you all believe that as bona fide believers in Christ today you are one spirit with the Lord? Do you have such a verse in your Bible? Do you realize that this is a fact revealed in the Bible, that we, the believers in Christ, are one spirit with Him? I do not only believe, I have been practicing this for years. I must tell you the truth, every time I am going to speak, my prayer is, "Lord, make it so real in the speaking that I am one spirit with You. It should not be just me speaking. Lord, it has to be me as one spirit with You speaking."

The Practical Way to Experience Christ

If the Lord is not the Spirit, how could we be one spirit with Him? If we are going to enjoy Christ, to experience Christ, first of all we have to realize that this Christ today is the anointed One, full of the Spirit, and that we are joined to Him as one spirit. Prior to the day we heard the gospel and were inspired to believe in the Lord Jesus, we did whatever we desired by ourselves. On the day we called on His name, we were saved and attached to the anointed One. We were made one spirit with our Savior. We may realize this fact, but the way we talk to others exposes whether or not we know the way to experience Christ. The right way to talk to others is to exercise our spirit. How do we exercise our spirit to contact the Lord? How do we practice this? According to my experience, the best way is to pray. To pray does not mean I have to go into my bedroom and close the door. I can pray spontaneously, "Lord, I am going to have a time with my brother. Lord, be with me. Be one with me." Before going to see my brother, I may have to go to the restroom. While I am going to the restroom, I can pray, "Lord, thank You, that You are my life, and You are my utterance." While I am in the restroom, I can pray. All the time I can pray. Then while the brother is in the next room, I pray, "Lord, be my talk. Lord, be my utterance. Even, Lord, be the sentences I am going to speak to my brother." We should practice this way all the time, realizing that the Lord is really one with us. Eventually, we will experience that this very Christ to whom God has attached us and with whom we have become one spirit is just our conversation. Our conversation with a brother is just Christ. Christ is so rich. He is our utterance, our thought, our word, and our expression. He is the very content of our conversation. He is the entire conversation. This is an experience of the riches of Christ.

Suppose that while you are speaking with a brother someone tells you that your wife wants you. You should begin to pray, "Lord, go with me. Go with me to meet my wife. Lord, be one spirit with me. I believe I'm one spirit with You. Lord, now is the time for You to prove it, so You have to be one with me to meet my wife. Lord, be my utterance, and be my eyes looking at my wife." Then you go to meet your wife. That meeting with your wife will be just Christ. While your wife may be so poor to you, you can still pray, "Lord, You are with me. Yes, Lord, this is Your situation." Then you will experience Christ as your patience, your endurance, your longsuffering, and your knowledge-surpassing love. If at that time your cousin is there and sees the situation, he would be surprised. He would admire the way you meet with your wife. In this way you will experience Christ when you meet with anyone in any kind of situation.

Even a young student has to learn how to experience Christ in the study of his lesson books. He may pray, "Lord, here is the lesson book, and tomorrow will be the final. Lord, prove that You are one spirit with me. Lord, read this book with me." If he does this, I assure you he will experience Christ as his understanding and as his wisdom to take in all the secrets of his lesson book. He will even experience Christ as his good memory. Then the next day when he takes the exam he does not need to be so pressed and so trembling. He just needs to pray, "Lord, I am one with You, and even one spirit with You. Not only in speaking, Lord, but even today in the classroom, taking the exam, I am one with You. Lord, make it so real. Make it so real to the angels. Make it so real to the entire universe that I am one with You." I assure you that he will experience Christ as his wisdom and quite often as his answer. This is the way. According to my observation, not many Christians experience Christ and enjoy Him today in this way. Even among us I am very concerned. Message after message has been given, but when we come to the practical things in our daily life, we are persons without Christ. In dealing with our wives, we are persons without Christ. In handling things, we are persons without Christ. In studying lesson books we are persons without Christ. We only practice being one spirit with the Lord at our ordained time for prayer. Even in most of the meetings, we do not practice this enough. I could not come to a meeting to speak to the saints without praying, "Lord, You have to vindicate that I am one spirit with You. I do not like to go there, Lord, to speak by myself. You have to go with me. You have to be my thought there. You have to be my feeling there in my speaking. You have to be the words, even the terms and the expressions of my speaking. Lord, even You have to be the speaking." Without such a prayer, I just would have no boldness to come to speak. Even though I have obtained a lot of knowledge of the Bible, I do not trust in that. Of course, we need Bible knowledge. But we have to speak not just with the words or verses from the Bible. In our speaking we must be one spirit with the Lord.

I beg you all to practice this. Do not take this as just another message. Since I came to this country, over three thousand messages have been given and printed. Yet the living of some of the saints makes me sorrowful. So many have heard and read the messages, and even participated in the trainings in which they were given. Yet in daily life the messages are gone. The messages could only be lived out when you have the practical experience of being one spirit with the Lord.

The reason why today's Christian meetings are so weak and so poor is because most of the Christians do not have this kind of experience of Christ. Every seeking saint is a genuine believer with a thirsty spirit created by God. Only God Himself, that is, the items of the riches of Christ, can satisfy people. So we must have the experience of Christ. Then when we come to the small meetings, we all can spontaneously say something and minister something that is Christ Himself. I recently read the testimony of a prominent government official in Taiwan. When he was close to forty years of age, he felt he was short of nothing physically, yet deep within him he was hungry for something of the real human life. At this time he and his wife visited many Christian meetings in Taipei, but felt that they had received nothing. One day, they were brought by some brothers to the meeting of the church in Taipei. On the first visit they realized that the Spirit of God was there. From that day, he was saved and began to attend the meetings. I just give you this testimony to show you what we need in our meetings. We must have something in spirit to pray or to sing or to say that can satisfy the hunger of the real seeking ones. This hunger is not in our mentality but in the depths of our being, that is, in our God-created and God-seeking spirit. For the home meetings we need the very Christ whom you and I experience.

How can the home meetings be strengthened, refreshed, and made new? How can they be so attracting, full of power, with might to uphold? There is no other way than to experience Christ. Just to have a list of all the items of the riches of Christ does not work. The only thing that works is what you have experienced. I hope that I have made this clear.

I hate to pass on to you another message of doctrine. I surely expect that you all would take this word and pray, "Lord, minute by minute I want to live a life praying to You all the time." This is why Paul says to "unceasingly pray" (1 Thes. 5:17). Years ago I did not understand what it meant to pray unceasingly. How could this be? Although I never received the proper instruction, gradually, by groping I touched the way. To pray unceasingly is just to pray all the day in all things. While I am writing, I pray, "Lord, be one with me in this writing. I am going to study a verse that is too deep. It is hard for me to apprehend. Lord, be one with me. I am studying a Greek word that is too deep. I have exhausted all the reference books, yet I cannot get the proper, right, spiritual significance. Lord, be one with me." Even when I am speaking, I have a praying spirit, "Lord, right now, be my utterance. Be my instant utterance, a present utterance, an utterance just for now, an utterance for some definite persons. Lord, be one sentence for a certain person I don't know." I prayed quite often in this way. The Lord answers and honors this kind of prayer. Quite often people have come to me and told me, "Brother Lee, tonight just one sentence out of your mouth caught me. That was exactly what I needed." We must be ones attached to God's Anointed and one spirit with Him. Then we will live such a daily life, in everything experiencing Him in specific ways.

In certain situations, you need humility, wisdom, forbearance, slowness, or quickness. If you pray in the way I have described, you will experience Christ as certain items. In one kind of environment, you will experience Him as your forbearance. In others, you will experience Him as your wisdom, your humility, or your longsuffering. With some weaker ones, you may experience Him as your sympathy, as your mercy, as your compassion. On all different occasions, and in everything, you will be one with Him and realize that He is one with you.

TO PREACH CHRIST AS THE GOOD NEWS

After this kind of experience we will come to the meeting with something of Christ. We will come to the meeting with the riches of Christ, not in our mind, but in our very being, because we have experienced Him and we have enjoyed Him. If we come to the meeting with these riches, we will surely have something to say. So we have to learn how to pick up the phrases, the terminology, and the expressions from the Bible. This is why we all have to study the Bible. We all may have something to say, yet if we do not have the expression, we have no way to utter it. For instance, if I am in an English-speaking meeting, yet I do not know any English, I may have something of Christ, but it would be impossible for me to utter it to you. Even if I have the knowledge of English, I also need the terminology, expressions, words, phrases, clauses, and sentences from the Bible. This is why we all have to read the Bible and the valuable spiritual books. From those books, spontaneously we will pick up many things. Even today in the elementary schools the teachers teach the young ones composition by reading. They have to read and read and read. In the same way we must have the experience and enjoyment of Christ's riches as an accumulation, a storage in us. Then we must read the Bible, and this will enrich our store. Also, we must read some spiritual books such as the life-studies to pick up not only the knowledge, but also the expressions and terminology to express what we have enjoyed of Christ. Then surely the home meetings will be rich. We will not be able to avoid it. We will have the riches and the utterance, and these riches and utterance will match the filling in our spirit and the strengthening into our inner man. If we have these four items, we will be the enriching, strengthening, refreshing, and renewing factors of the home meetings.

Now we are equipped with four things: the filling up in our spirit by the all-inclusive God; the strengthening into our inner man with might through the Holy Spirit; the experience, the enjoyment of Christ's riches; and the speaking. We have to realize that when we speak the experiences of the riches of Christ, our speaking is just the preaching of Christ as the gospel. Whatever we speak will be the gospel, the good news, the glad tidings. Acts 5:42 says, "They did not cease teaching and bringing the good news of Jesus as the Christ." In this verse, the Greek word translated "bringing the good news" is the same word translated "preach as the gospel" in Ephesians 3:8. In Ephesians 3:8 it is to preach the riches of Christ as the gospel; in Acts 5:42 it is to preach Jesus Christ Himself as the good news. This word in Greek really means something stronger than preach, so Darby renders it "announcing." Some other translations use the word "proclaim." The Greek word is a predicate indicating that we are announcing, we are proclaiming, we are preaching, we are speaking Christ and His riches as the gospel, as the glad tidings, as the good news. The Concordant Literal Version translates this word as "bringing the evangel." Evangel means the gospel, the glad tidings, the good news. Evangelize is the predicate. This is to evangelize with the riches of Christ. Evangelize means to preach, to proclaim, to announce something as the gospel.

Therefore, in all the home meetings, whatever we would speak would be the gospel, the good news to the hearers. I often have been hungry to get something in the home meetings. If one would speak Christ, that would be a glad tiding to me. If we are full of the enjoyment of the riches of Christ as we are going to a meeting, when we open our mouth, it will be the announcing of the riches of Christ as glad tidings to the attendants. This surely will enrich, strengthen, refresh, renew, and make our home meetings attracting and full of power to hold and to uphold.

CHAPTER FOUR

THE WAY TO PRACTICE THE HOME MEETINGS

Scripture Reading: Acts 5:42; 1 Cor. 12:1-3, 7-10; 14:1, 3, 4b, 12, 19, 23-26, 31; 2 Cor. 4:10-14

In this message we shall consider the way to practice the home meetings. The way to practice any meeting is to have first, mutuality, and second, speaking. These two things are very useful and prevailing in practicing any meeting.

MUTUALITY IN THE CHURCH MEETINGS

Due to the history of Christianity nearly all Christians today, including us, are not used to having mutuality in their meetings. Mostly in the so-called Christian services we see that one or two persons speak and the rest are just the audience. This is altogether not according to the scriptural teaching.

In the New Testament there are two main categories of Christian meetings. The first one is the meeting of the ministry, the meeting of the apostles, the meeting of any gifted persons such as Peter on the day of Pentecost. The meeting on the day of Pentecost was a meeting for the ministry. This kind of meeting cannot be considered as a meeting of the church and in the church. On the other hand, when 1 Corinthians 14 speaks of the meeting, it is referring to the meeting of the church and in the church. Verse 23 says, "If therefore the whole church comes together..." This is the meeting of the church and in the church. When we speak of the home meetings, we are surely referring to the meetings in the church and the meetings of the church.

In the preaching or teaching of the meeting of the

ministry, there is not much mutuality and not much speaking one to another. But according to 1 Corinthians 14, in the church meetings there is the basic need, the basic factor of mutuality. First Corinthians 14:23 says, "If therefore the whole church comes together..." Then verse 26 says that in this kind of meeting "each one has a psalm, has a teaching, has a revelation, has a tongue, has an interpretation." This shows us that the meeting of the church and in the church depends upon mutuality. There is always the feeling of one to another.

We must keep it well in mind that the home meetings surely are not meetings of any ministry. The home meetings are absolutely the meetings of the church and in the church. They depend one hundred percent upon mutuality. If there is no mutuality, there is no home meeting. To have a home meeting without mutuality causes that home meeting to lose its nature; it would not be a home meeting of the church. It might still be a home meeting but only of a small ministry where one speaks while all the rest listen. A speaker would be there with a small audience, but there would be no mutuality. First Corinthians 14 is the unique chapter in Paul's writings that teaches us something about the church meetings. In this unique chapter there is the basic factor of mutuality.

SPEAKING IN THE CHURCH MEETINGS

The second factor needed for the church meetings is speaking. If nobody speaks, that kills the church meeting. The lack of speaking kills the church meeting. The church meeting depends upon mutuality and speaking. The Scripture references for this message provide a base to fellowship concerning these two factors.

Acts 5:42 says, "And every day, in the temple and from house to house, they did not cease teaching and bringing the good news of Jesus as the Christ." This took place at the very beginning of the church life, following the day of Pentecost. After the thousands of new believers were saved, they met in the temple. The meeting in the temple was for the ministry, for Peter and John to minister, to speak, to preach, and to teach. Then verse 42 goes on to say that they met from house to house, in every house. What did they do there? They met to teach and to preach. No doubt they were teaching Christ, teaching the things concerning Christ. On the day of Pentecost after Peter's preaching, three thousand were saved and right away began to meet. Surely they did not talk about the Jewish religion. They surely talked about what they had heard in Peter's one message. They taught and they preached. They preached Jesus Christ as the glad tidings. In their meetings these two things were done; both involve speaking. To teach is to speak, and to preach is also to speak.

The Worship of the Living God Producing Speaking

First Corinthians 12:1 says, "Now concerning spiritual gifts, brothers, I do not want you to be ignorant." Paul was very wise, and he was a great teacher in a particular and profound way. When he touched the matter of spiritual gifts, he began in this way. In our version the word gifts is in italics. This indicates that this word is not in the Greek text. Paul only used the adjective form of *pneuma,* spiritual. This expression has bothered all the translators, but nearly all agree to fill in this word gifts.

Verse 2 continues, "You know that when you were of the nations," the Gentiles, "you were led away to dumb idols, however you were led." Paul was saying, "When you were Gentiles you had a kind of service. You had a kind of worship, and that was to idols. All the idols are dumb. This means that you Gentile people did not worship a speaking God. You worshipped idols who do not speak, dumb idols. Therefore you also became dumb. But when you worship the living God who is speaking, by this worship you will be made to speak." And this speaking is what Paul referred to by the word spiritual in verse 1. Although it is not wrong to insert the word gifts in verse 1, we have to study why Paul only wrote "spiritual." He was not only talking about spiritual gifts. When we touch or when we exercise the spiritual gifts, we touch a spiritual realm, we touch spiritual things, not only the gifts. We touch an entire situation which is pneumatic, an entire situation which is spiritual. Not only the gifts but also the situation, the environment, the atmosphere, the sphere, the realm, the items, and the contents are spiritual. I believe Paul used the word spiritual to indicate all these things. Whenever we touch or exercise spiritual gifts, a kind of environment, situation, or atmosphere is involved. The environment, the situation, the atmosphere, and even the persons should all be spiritual. We must be spiritual persons to exercise spiritual gifts. The environment should be spiritual, the atmosphere should be spiritual, the situation should be spiritual, what we speak should be spiritual, the speaker should be spiritual, and even our wording, utterances, and expressions all should be spiritual. Verses 2 and 3 show why this is so. When we were Gentiles, we worshipped the dumb idols. Nothing there was involved in the spiritual realm. There was no need of any spiritual environment, spiritual situation, spiritual atmosphere, spiritual person, spiritual words, spiritual elements, or spiritual items. We did not need anything spiritual because there was no speaking.

Because I was born into a Christian home, I do not believe that I had ever gone to an idol temple more than ten times. However, in 1935 a number of co-workers stayed on a scenic lake for two weeks, resting and studying the Word. While we were there, I visited the temples of the idols. At that time I saw that the worship of the idols was entirely dumb. From that day I understood Paul's word. In that kind of dumb worship there was no need of anything spiritual. But today we, the Christians, worship a living God who is speaking all the time. Our worship to Him surely makes us speakers. Those dumb worshippers do not have a Bible because their god is not the speaking God. But we have a thick volume of sixty-six books. There are so many pages because our God is the speaking God. Hebrews 1:1-3 says that our God speaks. He has spoken in the Old Testament and now He is speaking in the New Testament. He is the speaking God, so we Christians have to speak. If you are just a dumb worshipper, you do not look like a Christian. You do not practice as a Christian; you practice as a dumb worshipper, worshipping the dumb idols.

First Corinthians 12:2 and 3 say, "You know that when you were of the nations, you were led away to dumb idols, however you were led. Wherefore I make known to you that no one speaking in the Spirit of God says, Jesus is accursed; and no one can say, Lord Jesus, except in the Holy Spirit." Apparently the composition of these two verses is not logical, but if you get into the spiritual fact, Paul is more than logical. In verse 2 he says that to worship the idols makes you dumb. But when you come to God, God makes you speak. Then you speak, and the principle is that whenever you speak "Lord Jesus," you are in the Spirit. Time after time I saw some seeking Christians crying to the Lord, "Lord Jesus, I love You, Lord, but I feel empty. I have to be filled with Your Spirit." Right after such a one prayed some would come asking, "Have you received the Spirit?" Most of the ones asked answered, "No, I don't feel so." What would you say? The reason you would say no is because you do not feel that you have received the Spirit. But after reading verse 3 what would you say? You have cried, "Lord Jesus, I love You!" Have you received the Spirit? Yes! How do you know? "For the Bible tells me so." Do not say, "Because I feel so." I tell you, feeling is just like the weather. It comes, it goes, it fluctuates. It is like the air, the clouds, and the fog. It comes and it goes. Do not trust in your feeling. You must trust in the Word. "No one can say, Lord Jesus, except in the Holy Spirit." Can you say "Lord Jesus"? Try to say it from the depths of your being. "Lord Jesus!" Have you received the Spirit? "Yes, I have." How do you know? "The Bible tells me so." Where does it tell you? First Corinthians 12:3.

For the practice of the home meetings, we must learn to say, "Lord Jesus." Some brothers have advised me, "The strangers, the new ones are not used to our way. When they come in and hear someone say, 'Lord Jesus,' this will scare them away." If we all would say, "Lord Jesus," from our spirit, the strangers may not agree with what we say, yet after hearing it, something will be impressed into them. They may go away, but they will go away with a certain impression. If you do not say, "Lord Jesus," but instead you are so polite, so cultured, and so nice, the strangers would not be scared away. They would stay, yet they stay with an impression that is altogether meaningless. What they would say is, "Well, the meeting in that home is very polite, very nice, and all those people are so cultured." It would be better to have a meeting shouting, "O Lord Jesus," and scare people away with an impression of something. They would say, "I don't understand what that was, yet they had something there. Their speaking did something to me."

The Manifestation of the Spirit

Now from verse 3 we go to verse 7: "But to each one is given the manifestation of the Spirit for profit." In what way is the manifestation of the Spirit given? "To one through the Spirit is given a word of wisdom..." (v. 8). The number one manifestation of the Spirit is in the word of wisdom, not in miracles, not in healings, nor in tongue-speaking. The first manifestation is the word of wisdom, then, "to another a word of knowledge." The first manifestation is the word of wisdom and the second is the word of knowledge. This should impress us that in our home meetings we should be full of the word of wisdom and the word of knowledge. In the meetings the word of wisdom is on the top and the word of knowledge is not as high. Wisdom is mostly related to our spirit and knowledge is related to our mind. Wisdom comes from our spirit, where the Holy Spirit dwells. Knowledge mostly comes from the mind, where our thought is. But do not despise the word of knowledge. These are the two top manifestations of the Spirit in the Christian meetings.

Verse 9 says, "To a different one faith in the same Spirit, and to another gifts of healing in the one Spirit." The faith here is the kind of faith that can remove mountains. Verse 10 continues, "And to another operations of works of power." These are surely miracles. Three things are mentioned: faith to remove mountains, healing of diseases, and operations of works of power. Then it says, "And to another prophecy." To prophesy is also to speak. The word of wisdom is for speaking, the word of knowledge is for speaking, and prophecy is for speaking. Following this it says, "To another discerning of spirits." This is to discern what spirit is of God and what spirit is not of God. Then it says, "To a different one various kinds of tongues." We know all tongues are for speaking. It continues, "And to another interpretation of tongues." Interpretation of tongues is also for speaking. These are nine items of the manifestation of the Spirit. Five are for speaking: the word of wisdom, the word of knowledge, prophecy, tongues, and interpretation of tongues. These five all are for speaking. Then you have faith to remove some obstacles, the healing of diseases, the operations of the works of power, and the discerning of spirits.

Then 1 Corinthians 14:26 says, "What is it then, brothers? Whenever you come together, each one has a psalm, has a teaching, has a revelation." A psalm is not only for singing. Ephesians 5 tells us to speak one to another in psalms and hymns. Psalms are not only for singing, but also for speaking. Teachings surely are for speaking, and revelation is a kind of speaking. Verse 26 continues, "Has a tongue, has an interpretation." These are all for speaking. A psalm is for speaking and singing. A teaching is for speaking. A revelation is for speaking. A tongue is for speaking. An interpretation of a tongue is for speaking. All of the five items which are mentioned in relation to the Christian meetings are for speaking.

We have to study the word in the Lord's divine revelation very, very carefully. In chapter twelve, when Paul talks about the manifestation of the Spirit, he talks about nine items. Of the nine, four are miraculous things: faith, healing, miracles, and discerning of spirits. Five are for speaking: the word of wisdom, the word of knowledge, prophecy, tongues, and interpretation of tongues. Then when he talks about the meetings in chapter fourteen, he does not say a word concerning healing or concerning miracles. Instead, everything he says concerns speaking. You have to psalm. That means you have to speak or you have to sing. You need to voice it. Then you need to teach by speaking. You need to give a revelation by speaking. You need to speak a tongue, and interpret the tongue by speaking. It is all by speaking.

Then what are we to speak? Concerning all these kinds of speakings, Paul says in 14:1, "Pursue love, and desire earnestly spiritual gifts, but rather that you may prophesy." The word prophesy both in Hebrew and in Greek, in both the Old and New Testaments, denotes three things. First, to prophesy is to speak for God, to tell people something for God. Second, it is to speak forth God, to tell something forth concerning God. Third, it is to foretell, to tell beforehand that something will happen. The third denotation is a matter of prediction. Today many Christians understand this word prophesy only to mean predict or foretell. But if you read 1 Corinthians 14, you can understand that the word prophesy in this chapter does not refer mainly to foretelling, but rather to speaking forth Christ and to speaking for Christ. To prophesy in this chapter is just to speak forth the things concerning God and to speak for God, or you may say, to speak forth the things concerning Christ, and to speak for Christ. Then verse 3 says, "But he who prophesies speaks to men for building up and encouragement and consolation." This is surely not a prediction, but rather a kind of speaking in the word of wisdom or in the word of knowledge to build others up and to encourage, comfort, and console others.

Then verse 4 says, "He who prophesies builds up the church." To speak forth Christ and to speak for Christ builds up the church. Verses 23 through 26 say, "If therefore the whole church comes together in one place, and all speak in tongues, and the unlearned or unbelievers enter, will they not say that you are insane? But if all prophesy and some unbeliever or unlearned person enters, he is convicted by all, he is judged by all; the secrets of his heart become manifest; and so falling on his face, he will worship God, reporting that God is really among you. What is it then, brothers? Whenever you come together, each one has a psalm, has a teaching, has a revelation, has a tongue, has an interpretation." Each one has! You have a psalm. I have a teaching. He has a revelation. Another has a tongue. And a fifth one has an interpretation. This is mutuality. A basketball team has five players. If, however, one player keeps the ball to himself and never lets it go, that is not mutuality, but rather individuality. The principle is the same in the meetings. We must practice mutuality. If during a meeting only one person speaks the entire time, everyone will leave feeling poor. But if everyone speaks mutually the meeting will be very much enriched.

The word tongue in verse 26 means a real tongue that

can be interpreted. The tongue must be a dialect that bears a certain meaning that can be translated. In Acts 2:6 we can see that tongue-speaking was the speaking of a dialect. All the hearers were amazed that they could hear in their own language: "We hear them speaking in our tongues the great things of God" (Acts 2:11). First Corinthians chapters twelve and fourteen are also portions in the New Testament which talk about tongue-speaking. In this portion Paul says that if one speaks in tongues in the meeting, there must also be an interpretation: "If anyone speaks in a tongue, let it be by two, or at the most three, and in turn, and let one interpret; but if there is no interpreter, let him be silent in the church, and let him speak to himself and to God" (1 Cor. 14:27-28). These verses show that any tongue spoken in a meeting must be a distinct dialect.

Once I was invited to speak to a Pentecostal group. I stayed with them for quite a few days. While I was there, I observed a speaking in tongues and an interpretation of it; however, the interpretation was several times longer than the speaking in tongues. Even the pastor admitted that this was not genuine. Later, I observed one person repeating the same tongue-speaking on three occasions, yet each interpretation was greatly different. This kind of tongue speaking is altogether false. When we speak of tongues, we refer to the genuine tongues. Not just a sound produced with the tongue, but syllables which are meaningful that can compose a language. This is a genuine tongue. This is what the Bible reveals.

In 1 Corinthians 12, nine different items are mentioned as the manifestation of the Spirit. The first is the word of wisdom and the second is the word of knowledge, but the last two are tongue-speaking and interpretation of tongues. Then in 1 Corinthians 14:26 there are five things related to the meetings, there is firstly a psalm for speaking and singing, then a teaching for speaking, then a revelation for speaking. These are the first three. Then the last two are tongues and interpretation. In Paul's writings, tongues and their interpretation are at the tail of every list, but today's practice makes the tail the head. In the Pentecostal movement, they make tongues not only the head, but nearly everything. The most important thing in a Christian meeting is not tongue-speaking; it is the speaking of the word of wisdom, the speaking of the word of knowledge, the speaking of a teaching, and the speaking of a revelation that can reveal something, that can instruct people, and that can build up the saints and the church.

Believing and Therefore Speaking

For the home meetings we need mutuality and speaking for the building up. But many of you will say, "Brother Lee, we just don't have the gift of speaking. Thank the Lord that He has given you such a gift that you can speak for many hours at a time. But I cannot do this. I am not so gifted. I do not have the speaking gift." Due to our feeling that we are unable to speak in the meetings, we need to consider 2 Corinthians 4:10-14. In these verses Paul speaks about Christ's death and His resurrection in a subjective way, in a way that identifies us with Christ's death and resurrection. Verses 10-12 say, "Always bearing about in the body the putting to death of Jesus, that the life also of Jesus might be manifested in our body. For we who live are always being delivered unto death for Jesus' sake, that the life also of Jesus might be manifested in our mortal flesh. So then death operates in us, but life in you." How could Paul speak in this way? In verse 13 he gives us the secret: "And having the same spirit of faith..." What is the "spirit of faith"? Dean Alford in his *New Testament for English Readers* states that the spirit of faith is "not distinctly the Holy Spirit,—but still not merely a human disposition: the indwelling Holy Spirit penetrates and characterizes the whole renewed man." Vincent in his *Word Studies in the New Testament* says, "Spirit of faith: not distinctly the Holy Spirit, nor, on the other hand, a human faculty or disposition, but blending both." The spirit of faith is the mingling of the Holy Spirit with our human spirit. We must exercise such a spirit to believe and to speak the things we have experienced of the Lord, especially His death and resurrection. Faith is in our spirit, which is mingled with the Holy Spirit, not in our mind. Doubts are in our mind. The "spirit" in verse 13 indicates that it is by the mingled spirit that the apostles live a crucified life in resurrection for carrying out their ministry. This spirit of faith was Paul's secret.

Verse 13 continues, "And having the same spirit of faith, according to that which is written, I believed, therefore I spoke; we also believe, therefore also we speak." Do not believe your feelings. Do not believe your habit. We have to exercise our spirit to believe that we have experienced something of the Lord. Have we not experienced the death of Christ? Have we not experienced the resurrection of Christ? We have! Now we need to exercise our spirit to speak. First, we must exercise our spirit to believe what we have experienced; then we must exercise our spirit to speak what we believe. We all need to speak in this way.

Perhaps one would say, "Well, you know I am just a sister. I don't know if I have something to speak about. Maybe I don't." This is a lie from the usurping enemy. The enemy has been usurping us, the Christians, for years. He has made us all dumb. We have gone for years without speaking in the meetings. Now is the time for us to revolt, to stand up and declare to the enemy, "Get away from me, Satan. I don't believe that. I am not dumb. I am not serving a dumb idol. I am worshipping a speaking God and He is speaking within me. His speaking Spirit is mingled with my spirit. Now I can exercise my spirit to believe that I have experienced Christ. I have experienced something of Christ. I have experienced Him in His resurrection as my patience, as my endurance. I have experienced Him as life. Christ is my life. I have experienced this, so I exercise my spirit to believe in this and to speak what I have experienced." This is the secret of speaking.

In the following messages I will tell you how to get the terminology, terms, expressions, phrases, utterances, and even sentences for your speaking. But in this message we have to pick up the matter of the mutuality as the factor in our meetings for speaking. The secret is to believe that we have experienced something of Christ. Then we have to exercise our spirit to speak what we believe. This speaking will build up the saints and the church. When we speak, we speak by exercising our spirit. We exercise our spirit to believe what we have experienced of Christ and to utter what we believe. Try to practice this.

CHAPTER FIVE

THE WAY TO SPEAK IN THE HOME MEETINGS

Scripture Reading: Num. 11:29; 1 Cor. 12:13; 14:1, 31; Col. 3:16; 1 Tim. 6:3

In the previous message we saw that in order to practice the home meetings, mutuality and speaking must be stressed very much. In this message we shall see how to speak in the home meetings. The matter of speaking is a wonderful thing. Suppose that among mankind, in human society, there were not such a thing as speaking. How would that be? According to history, human culture is mainly dependent upon speaking. Without language and speaking there could be no culture. Without language there would be no possibility for any kind of communication.

GOD'S DESIRE FOR ALL HIS PEOPLE TO PROPHESY

Recently, I discovered that not only in the New Testament, but in the Old Testament as well, God expressed His desire concerning His people. In Numbers 11 Moses was burdened with the care of the people of Israel, who numbered about two million. God told Moses to call the seventy elders out of their camps and gather them into His tabernacle. When the elders came, the Spirit of God descended upon them, and they all began to prophesy. They began to be prophets speaking for God (Num. 11:25). Two of them were not among the ones around the tabernacle. Even they began to speak because the Spirit of the Lord was also upon them. When Joshua knew this he became unhappy and said, "My lord Moses, forbid them" (Num. 11:28). However, Moses replied,

"Enviest thou for my sake? would God that all Jehovah's people were prophets, and that Jehovah would put his Spirit upon them" (Num. 11:29). This verse corresponds exactly with Paul's word in 1 Corinthians 14:31: "For you can all prophesy."

Naturally speaking, when we say the English word prophesy, we understand this to mean to predict, to foretell, to tell of something before it happens. Yes, prophesy in English does bear this denotation. But in the two Biblical languages, Hebrew and Greek, the word for prophesy means not primarily to predict, but to speak for God. If you speak for yourself, that is not to prophesy. But if you speak for God, this is to prophesy. Not only so, it also means to speak forth God. That means you speak God out. In your speaking you not only speak for God, but also in this kind of divine speaking you speak God forth into others. You speak God out to others. Of course, this word prophesy, both in Hebrew and in Greek, also means to foretell, but in the writings of the prophets Isaiah, Jeremiah, and Ezekiel, there is very little foretelling. In Isaiah, a book of sixty-six chapters, perhaps all the foretellings, all the predictions, could only comprise the equivalent of one chapter. But the other sixty-five chapters do speak for God and speak forth God. It is the same with Jeremiah. In the fifty-two chapters of Jeremiah there is very little foretelling or predicting. The greater part of Jeremiah is a speaking for God and a speaking forth of God. It is the same with Ezekiel and even with the minor prophets. The greatest prophet in the Old Testament was Moses. Moses spoke so much in his five books of the Old Testament, the Pentateuch. Here there are not many predictions. Rather, most of Moses' speaking or writing is a speaking for God and a speaking forth of God. If you are going to know God, you have to read these five books from Genesis through Deuteronomy. When you read Moses' five books, you do have the sense that these books are speaking forth God into you. In today's terms, these books are dispensing the very God which they reveal into our being. This is not only the speaking for God, but also the speaking forth of God.

In the Pentecostal movement I heard a lot of Pentecostal

foretellings, yet I never saw one fulfillment. The so-called predictions or foretellings in today's Pentecostal movement are mostly false. In China from 1932 I began to study the Pentecostal movement. I heard the prophecies and I saw what followed, but I did not see any fulfillment. Then, twenty-four years ago, I came to this country and was invited to some of the Pentecostal meetings to speak there. I saw how they predicted and how nothing happened. They always opened their prophecy with "My people, time is short," and they always ended it with "thus saith the Lord."

In their prophesying they never quoted anything from the New Testament. They always quoted some phrases or verses from the Old Testament, mostly from Isaiah. However, in the New Testament, when the Lord Jesus spoke in the four Gospels, He never ended His speaking with "thus saith the Lord." Furthermore, in none of Paul's fourteen Epistles did he say, "Thus saith the Lord." Rather, he said, "I have no commandment of the Lord, but I give my opinion" (1 Cor. 7:25). He did not say, "Thus saith the Lord," but he wrote, "I give my opinion as having received mercy of the Lord to be faithful." Then at the end of 1 Corinthians 7 he said, "I think that I also have the Spirit of God." That means, "even though I told you my opinion, yet I think I have the Spirit of God." He did not say, "Thus saith the Holy Spirit." From this you can see that this kind of Pentecostal prophesying brings us all backward to the Old Testament, forgetting what is revealed in the New Testament.

In the New Testament, especially in Paul's writings in 1 Corinthians 12 and 14, the word prophesy is used not mainly with the meaning to predict. Rather, it is used strongly with the meaning to speak for Christ and to speak forth Christ. In 1 Corinthians 12:3 Paul says, "No one speaking in the Spirit of God says, Jesus is accursed; and no one can say, Lord Jesus, except in the Holy Spirit." To say "Lord Jesus" is to prophesy. You have to put verse 3 of chapter twelve together with verse 1 of chapter fourteen. In 14:1 Paul says, "Pursue love, and desire earnestly spiritual gifts, but rather that you may prophesy." To prophesy is just to speak the Lord Jesus, to speak for Jesus, or to speak forth Christ. This is to speak in the New Testament denotation.

Not just in our meetings, but even in our daily life, we must be people all the time speaking Christ, all the time speaking for Christ, and all the time speaking forth Christ. If I come to you and do not speak a bit of Christ, but instead just talk with you about schools, about the world situation, about Taiwan, about Hong Kong, about your city, and this and that, I am doing what the worldly people do. Whenever and wherever we open up our mouths, we speak Christ, we speak for Christ, and we speak forth Christ. In Acts 1:8 the Lord Jesus told us clearly that we all are His witnesses: "But you shall receive power when the Holy Spirit has come upon you, and you shall be My witnesses." A witness is a speaking one, one who only speaks things concerning the one he is testifying. We are His witnesses and we have to speak Him, speak for Him, and speak forth Him on every occasion. Even when young ones go to their grandparents, they should not speak that much concerning other things. They should speak Christ, speak for Christ, and speak forth Christ. This is to prophesy. I do not think we all can prophesy in the sense of predicting; I cannot nor would I like to. But we all can speak; we all can prophesy in the sense of speaking Christ or speaking for Christ. I have been speaking for Him, speaking forth Him, and speaking Him directly to others for over fifty years. You also can do this. Paul says, "You can all prophesy" (1 Cor. 14:31). You all can speak for Christ, speak forth Christ, and speak Christ. Speak Christ all the day. Surely if you love the Lord and you have good fellowship with Him every day, then every day in your fellowship with the Lord you are spontaneously anointed and filled up within. You are anointed without and filled within. Spontaneously you have a lot to say, you have a lot to speak. To speak what? To speak Christ, to speak for Christ, and to speak forth Christ. This is a strong proof that we Christians should be this kind of speaking people. We all have to realize that it is God's desire that we Christians should be a speaking people, and we have to try our best to fulfill His desire.

THE SPIRIT UPON US AND WITHIN US FOR OUR SPEAKING

According to the principle revealed in the Scriptures, to speak God, to speak forth Christ, and to speak for Christ, surely we need the Spirit. Without the Spirit, we would not speak, and even if we would speak, we would feel shameful. When you talk about science, geography, history, or the political situation, the more you talk, the more you feel quite proud. There is no restriction or frustration in speaking about these things. But whenever you speak about Jesus, the feeling of shame follows right away. It seems hard to open up your mouth to speak about Jesus to people. Unless we have the Spirit, it is really hard for us to speak Christ. But when we are filled with the Spirit, we become crazy; we like to speak things concerning Christ to people.

For this reason, in the Old Testament, when the seventy were going to prophesy, the Spirit of God descended upon them. As genuine Christians, believers in Christ, do we still need the Spirit of God to descend upon us? If you say, "Yes," then you are in the Old Testament. In the Old Testament the incarnation and crucifixion were not accomplished. There was no resurrection of Christ and no ascension, so there was no breathing of the processed life-giving Spirit into God's people, and there was no outpouring of the processed Triune Spirit upon God's people. However, in the New Testament, incarnation, crucifixion, resurrection, and ascension have been fully accomplished. Today our Lord is the processed God. He went through all the necessary processes and in His resurrection He breathed Himself as the life-giving Spirit into His disciples, into us. He does not need to do it again. He died for us once for all. He does not need to die again for you and me particularly; such a thought is wrong. In the same principle, He does not need to breathe Himself into you and me particularly, because He has breathed Himself into all His disciples as the life-giving Spirit on the day of resurrection (John 20:22). Hallelujah! Not only so, in His ascension He has poured Himself out as the economical, processed Triune Spirit upon all the members of His Body. All the members of His Body, in ancient or in modern time, Greek or Jew, slave or free, were once for all baptized in one Spirit. We were baptized in one Spirit and now we all are given to drink of this Spirit (1 Cor. 12:13).

Nearly all of us have the faith that the Spirit is in us. When you are going to argue with your wife, someone inside you would not let you do it. That someone is the indwelling Spirit. We know that the Spirit is in us and we have the faith to say this. We also need the assurance that the Spirit is upon us. The impact for speaking comes from the Spirit who is right now upon us. If I did not have the assurance that I have the Spirit upon me, I would not be speaking now. I believe that my impact comes from this Spirit who is right now upon me.

Over forty years ago I did a lot of preaching in large gospel meetings. One morning when I spoke to a large congregation, I said something to the young junior high students. I told them that even though they considered that they had not committed sin, at least on one occasion one had stolen the chalk from their school and taken it back home. I did not know while I was speaking that there was a student there who had done exactly that. Later, I found out that in the meeting there was a young boy about thirteen years of age, a son of a widowed sister. This boy, although quite smart, would not listen to his mother to believe in the Lord Jesus. Yet he came to the meeting that morning, and when he heard me speaking, he thought to himself, "That is nothing." Then I asked, "Is that nothing?" It was quite strange that I should have spoken in this way. I said, "You drew circles upon the floor with the stolen chalk." That shocked him. He thought, "Who told this man that I did this?" What I had spoken was altogether a clear description of what he had done. It was through this that he repented. Do you think that was me? Actually, this shows that when I was speaking, the Spirit was not only within me but also upon me to carry out the speaking. This happened in my speaking a number of times.

OUR FAITH, OUR SPIRIT, AND THE HOLY SPIRIT

Now you all have to practice the same thing. In the home meetings you all have to learn to speak by faith. This faith, as we have seen in the last message, is wrapped up with the spirit. This spirit is not merely our spirit nor merely the Holy Spirit, but is altogether a mingled spirit. We know today that we have a mingled spirit within us, the Holy Spirit mingling with our spirit. Whenever we would not care for the environment or the circumstances, but would only care for what the Bible says, we exercise our faith. Whenever we exercise our faith, our spirit is involved and the Holy Spirit is also there. Here we have three things: our faith, our spirit, and the Holy Spirit. We all must learn to speak in any kind of meeting by faith, by our spirit, and by the Holy Spirit. Actually, the three things are just one. When we speak by faith, we exercise our spirit. When we exercise our spirit, the Holy Spirit is moving in our spirit. This makes a difference. Speak what the Bible says. If we would exercise our believing ability, faith will be there. When we speak what the Bible says, the spirit is there and the Holy Spirit is also there. This makes our speaking so living.

Today we are not in the Old Testament times. We are not in that economy. We are in the New Testament economy. In this economy God has poured out His Spirit upon us already. This Spirit is both dwelling within us and resting upon us. He is like the blowing wind and the air. If we would just open the window, we would have the blowing and we would have the air. In the New Testament dispensation the wind is blowing all the day and the air is here all the time. We have to believe this according to the Bible. Therefore, we have the Spirit within us and the Spirit upon us as well. Now we are just those baptized in the Spirit and drinking the one Spirit.

In the New Testament, especially in the Acts, the baptism of the Spirit refers to the descending of the Spirit upon the believers. The baptism in the Spirit and the descending of the Spirit both refer to the same fact. In the Old Testament the word baptism or baptize was not used, but the thought of descending is there. The Spirit of Jehovah descended upon His people. This descending of the Spirit is like the baptism of the Spirit. This baptism has been fully accomplished and the issue now is resting upon us. We have to believe this. Not only so, we have to practice this. Even at home when you talk to your family concerning Christ, you have to exercise your faith, and you have to exercise your spirit. You have to believe that the Spirit is upon you as well as in you. Even when you are talking to your children, you have to talk in this way. Regretfully, we feel that it is only when we are to release a message that we need faith, the spirit, and the Holy Spirit. We do not feel this need when we talk to our wife, to our husband, to our parents, or to our children. Our speaking to them in this way, without faith, may put them to sleep. But the divine speaking could never make people sleepy. Rather it stirs up people. If we would practice the divine speaking, we would become accustomed to it. Then on the Lord's Day we would come to the meeting speaking. We would not come to the meeting silent. We would be used to speaking the divine speaking. In this way we would speak with faith, with the spirit, and with the Holy Spirit. This is the right way.

I have a heavy burden because I feel it is hard for me to stir up your heart and turn your mentality to pay full attention to this matter. In the meeting you nod your head to me but when you leave, you just forget about it. You do not practice this. Would you promise that from now on you would begin to practice this all the time? If you do not have anyone to speak to, you can just speak to the air. Maybe some angels would be there and some demons would be there listening to your speaking. Anyhow, just speak in this way. Speak, speak, speak. Speak by faith. When you do this by the exercise of your believing ability, your spirit is involved and the Holy Spirit is also involved. Then your speaking becomes divine. It is a kind of divine speaking. Those who are silent in the meetings may say, "Brother Lee, don't blame me. You have to blame God who created me this way. This is my makeup. I didn't do it, God did it. Brother Lee, you have to thank God for His mercy that He created you in this way—speaking, speaking, speaking all the time. I was not created by God in this way and I cannot speak." To say this is to annul Paul's word. Paul says you all can prophesy.

THE WORD OF CHRIST DWELLING IN US FOR OUR SPEAKING

You may have the faith, you may have the spirit, and you

may have the Holy Spirit as well, but when you try to speak, you feel you have nothing to speak about. Of course, you say you are short of experiences. That is right, but I would say you are short not only of experiences but also of the word of Christ. Colossians 3:16 says, "Let the word of Christ dwell in you richly." You have to notice that in this verse Paul says, "Let the word of Christ dwell in you." This kind of tone indicates that the word of Christ is here waiting for you to let it come into you. It seems that a Person is waiting here, waiting for you to let Him in. Years ago when I read this verse, I did not agree with this kind of tone. Why does Paul say, "Let the word of Christ dwell in you"? The indication here is that today the living word of Christ is waiting for you to let it in. This word is personified as a living Person. You do not say, "Let the table dwell in your room." The table cannot dwell because it is lifeless. Anything that can dwell in your home must be a living person. A lifeless thing cannot dwell. Paul says, "Let the word of Christ dwell in you," and the New Testament tells us that Christ is the Word. Not only so, the Spirit also is the Word (Eph. 6:17). The Word, Christ, the Spirit, and God—these four actually are one. These are four synonyms referring to this same one Person. God is Christ, Christ is the Spirit, the Spirit is the Word, and the Word is God, Christ, and the Spirit. Therefore, the Word is a living Person. Paul does not say the word of some other one or other thing. He says the word of Christ. Surely this is the organic Word, the living Word, the Word which exists as a living Person. This Word is waiting to get into you. You have to open up yourself and let Him in.

Colossians 3:16 continues, "teaching and admonishing one another in psalms, hymns, and spiritual songs." If you read this verse carefully, you can see some controversy here. First it is the Word, yet eventually it is a psalm or a hymn. The principle is this: if you do not speak a certain word very many times, that word could never be a psalm or a song. Whatever becomes a psalm or a hymn has to be a word that you have been speaking once, twice, three times, four times, many, many times—then that word will become a psalm. You cannot write a song unless you compose it with the words spoken by you repeatedly. The same word spoken by you again and again eventually becomes a poem, a song, a hymn, or a psalm. For instance, Hymn #499 in our hymnal says, "Oh, what a life! Oh, what a peace! The Christ who's all within me lives." This is poetry composed by me. I had been speaking this for years. "The Christ who's all within me lives. With Him I have been crucified....Now it's no longer I that live, but Christ the Lord within me lives." I had been speaking the next verse also. "Christ now is being formed in me. His very nature and life divine in my whole being inwrought shall be. All that I am came to an end, and all of Christ is all to me." I had been speaking this, so eventually it became a song. This indicates that we have to let the word of the Lord dwell in us to such an extent that it eventually becomes a song, a hymn, or a psalm. Psalms are long poems, hymns are shorter ones, and spiritual songs are the shortest.

The word of Christ is personified; it is a living Person who is waiting for you to let Him in. Once you let Him in, He becomes your speaking again and again. Eventually, this speaking will become poetry with rhythm and rhyme. Sometimes, when you begin to speak for the Lord, you feel awkward. When you speak the worldly things, which you have been speaking for many years, you can utter them like a song, like a psalm with rhythm and rhyme. But after being saved only two weeks, when you began to speak Christ, it was somewhat awkward. We have to let the word of Christ as a Person dwell in us and we have to speak this word fluently until we become accustomed to it and it becomes like poetry in our speaking. We all have to learn to speak Christ and we have to learn to become accustomed to speaking Christ. We need to become accustomed to it to such an extent that whatever we say will be a kind of poetry—a song, a psalm, and a hymn. Likewise, we speak the healthy words (1 Tim. 6:3).

In conclusion, we must first realize that God desires us to speak. He desires all His people to prophesy. Second, to speak we need the Spirit. This Spirit is upon us and this Spirit is within us. Hallelujah! We were baptized in the Spirit; therefore, the Spirit is upon us. We are also drinking the Spirit; therefore, the Spirit is in us. We have the Spirit. Now we just need to exercise, to amen what the Bible says. The

Bible says the Spirit is upon us. We say, "Amen." The Bible says the Spirit is within us. We say, "Amen." We exercise such a spirit of faith to realize that we are really in the spirit, and that the Spirit is upon us and is also within us. When I speak, He is speaking in my speaking. We have to practice this all the day long. If there is no one to speak to, just speak to the angels in the air or the demons around you. Let the living word of Christ come in and dwell in you. Then speak Christ, not in the common, ordinary, worldly expressions, but with Himself as the Word. We have to learn the spiritual terminology, the spiritual phrases, clauses, and even the spiritual sentences. This is why I pointed out earlier that it is better to pick up a hymnal to recite some hymns. This will help you to utter something. Along with this, of course, we need our daily experiences. But I assure you, if you are such a person to exercise speaking by faith with the spirit and with the Holy Spirit, spontaneously you will experience Christ. You will experience Christ all day long, not only in big things, but especially in all the small things: how to comb your hair, how to dress yourself, how to put on your shoes, what kind of shoes you should buy, and what color you should select. In all the small things you will experience Christ. Then you will have an accumulation of the rich experience of Christ in you, and whenever you come to the meeting you are used to speaking and you just speak. You speak Christ, you speak for Christ, and you speak forth Christ with the living Word. If we all would do this, all these small meetings will be in the third heaven. This will be very attractive, even attracting. This will hold people and preserve them, and this will produce the increase and the growth in life. This is the proper way. I hope that you all would be attracted by this kind of practice so that the church would have a way to go on among us in His recovery.

Chapter Six

SPEAKING IN THE WAY OF LIFE

Scripture Reading: Col. 3:16; John 6:63b; 1 Tim. 6:3; 3:2; 5:17

THE SHORTAGE OF BUILDING AND LIGHT

The subject of this message is quite simple—speaking in the way of life—yet I do have a heavy burden. Today we are here at nearly the end of the twentieth century. We have studied church history, and we have read the biographies and classic writings of the Lord's servants through the past centuries. Even we ourselves have passed through Christianity for a long time and we have experienced very much of the church life. Today we are in the United States, which is the leading country of Christianity, full of Christian activities, Christian denominations, Christian groups, and so forth. In spite of all this, if you were to look at the present situation, you would be mostly disappointed. What could you see today? You could see the Catholic church, the big denominations, all the middle-sized Christian groups, the small ones, and the churches in the Lord's recovery. It is not very encouraging. Rather, every situation is quite disappointing, or at least somewhat disappointing.

The disappointment is mainly in two things. First, there is no building. After twenty centuries of Christian history, what is the issue today? The issue apparently is just big Christendom, which still remains here. Including the Catholic members, the Christians today comprise at least one-fourth of the world population. Among so many Christians, many are false ones, nominal ones, yet still a good number are real ones. Among the genuine ones, however, we could see very little building.

Second, you see ignorance in today's Christianity. Most of the Catholic members just follow their kind of superstition. They believe that a statue in front of the cathedral can do something for them. This is superstition. They also believe superstitious stories about angelic activities which are said to have occurred centuries ago in Spain, France, and Italy. Things like this just fill up Catholicism. In the Protestant denominations you could also see ignorance, even with the Lutheran church, which is established on the belief in justification by faith. If you were to ask a devout member of the Lutheran church to give you a short word on justification by faith, I do not think he could do it well. This is a strong indication of ignorance. Actually, this is not just ignorance but darkness. Even among the genuine believers you could not find many who are in the light.

Is there any building in today's Pentecostalism? Is there any light? Rather, I would say, the superstitious waves have also invaded Pentecostalism. They like to talk about dreams, to speak great prophecies, and to practice healings. I have attended some healing campaigns and I did not see any genuine healing. All I saw was a performance with some kind of artificial healing. The leaders knew this was false, yet everybody believed in these healings. This is superstition without any building or enlightenment.

Now, let us consider our situation. Forget about others and let us criticize ourselves. Are you built up? How much have you been built up? I must admit that we are better than nothing. If you compare us with those with nothing, you have to say that we have something. How about enlightenment? For the past eleven and a half years, we have had two trainings annually. In each training thirty messages were spoken and printed. Many of you have hundreds of life-study messages on your bookshelves, but I do not think ten percent of these messages are in your heart and in your mind. Our situation is just like a housewife whose husband bought a lot of groceries for her, but she never cooked them.

THE NEED FOR COOKING AND TEACHING

In October, 1984, I fully realized that we must have a

thorough change in our way of meeting, or in our way of taking care of the saints in the meetings. We have to change. I call the old way the "lazy way." If the groceries are bought and stored, yet there is no labor to cook them, that is just laziness.

Whether a nation is strong or weak mainly depends upon its people, its citizens. If you have strong, proper families, surely you will have strong and proper citizens. Then the country will be strong. If you do not have proper families, it is hard for you to have a proper society. The families are the real and basic factors to build up the society and to build up the country. To build up a proper and strong family, first you need to take care of the feeding, and second the education. If the wife does not take care of the children properly in these two things, in eating and education, you should not expect that this family will be proper. The future of this family will be pitiful. The wife, the mother of the family, has to labor in cooking. You can spend four hours to cook a meal or you can spend ten minutes to cook a meal. A proper meal is both nourishing and tasty. It also should not be too expensive. These are the principles you have to keep. To do such a thing, you need to labor. You cannot go to the grocery store and pick up the things in a light way. As the wife, the mother of the family, you have to labor very much. I would propose to you that for breakfast you need to labor one hour. This includes purchasing, preparation, cooking, and presentation. For lunch you need at least an hour and a half, and for dinner, at least two hours. You may say, "We can't make it! I have to go to work, I have to study, and do many other things." The choice is up to you. If you want to gradually commit suicide, not only for yourself, but also for all your children, it is up to you. It depends on what you want. Do you want a healthy family? You may argue that there are not enough hours in the day, but I would say, "If there's a will, there's a way." Young people surely can squeeze their sleeping time from eight hours to seven hours. Just squeeze a little bit, this way and that way, but do not squeeze the cooking time nor the eating time. If you cook with too little time and you eat too fast, surely you would not be healthy. How good you are as a wife or as a mother is measured by the time you spend cooking. Any unhappiness in a family is mostly due to inadequacy in cooking.

In Christianity the way to take care of the members of a church is the lazy way. There just is not much cooking. I hope that all the leading ones, not just the elders, but all those concerned for the church, those with a sincere concern for the Lord's recovery, including myself, will have a turn from the old way. Since you are the housewives and the mothers in the church, you need to labor in the word and in teaching (1 Tim. 5:17). Paul says the overseers must be "apt to teach" (1 Tim. 3:2). This phrase does not mean to teach accidentally. It is to teach in a habitual way. Apt to teach implies a habit, a desire, or an appetite to teach. The overseers, the elders in the church, should be like this, apt to teach.

In 1 Timothy 5, Paul says that the elders should labor to the extent that they could not work at a job. "Let the elders who take the lead well be counted worthy of double honor, especially those who labor in word and teaching" (v. 17). The double honor includes financial supply because they are laboring so much; they are fully occupied with the need of the church. For a human being to do anything, there is the need of time. If you are fully occupied physically and mentally, you can do nothing. "Labor" in this verse is to labor in the word and in teaching.

According to this yardstick, all the elders are not so diligent. They do not labor in the Word much, and they do not labor in teaching adequately. The elders are always afraid to be charged to speak, because to speak is a hard thing. Yet you have to realize in our practice of the church life, the speaking of the elders has been mainly to give a message. To give a message is easy, but to take care of the church as an elder or to do some cooking all the time for the saints is hard.

In the elders' training held in February, 1984, I told the elders how they should take care of the meetings. As an elder you should not go to the meeting to occupy the entire meeting with your speaking. That is not the way to build up the church. The way to build up the church is to gather the saints together, encouraging them to speak, even charging them to speak one by one. Every time you attend a big meeting or a small meeting, you should labor very much before the meeting in the Word. You should get yourself equipped and prepared with something before you go to the meeting. You should let all the saints have the meeting. In case they do not have anything to open the meeting with, after just a few minutes you have to serve them a cooked dish. That means you have to give them a living word lasting less than ten minutes that is rich, enlightening, stirring, and watering. Then you should turn the meeting to all the saints. Maybe a few will continue to say something. After that, it may stop. Then you have to do something again to serve them with another dish. By this way, you will train all the saints to function in the meetings. This is not so easy; it requires a lot of preparation. This needs a lot of laboring. According to my observation, to take care of a church as an elder is harder than just to go out and hold conferences. To hold conferences is quite an enjoyment, but to stay in a locality to take care of at least four or five meetings a week is not so easy. To take care of the church is a heavy burden, and the heaviest point of this burden is to take care of the meetings. This is just like a mother or a wife in a home. For the mother to take care of the cooking for her family is a really hard job.

Yet, you have to realize that in a family such a good mother has to do another necessary thing, that is, to teach her children. You must not only send the children to school, but also take care of the children in doing their homework. When they come home with their school lesson books, you have to charge them to work on those lesson books, and you have to teach them. Then you can expect that your children will be reared in the proper way both physically and mentally. Physically they get the proper home-cooked food from you, and they also receive the proper education. To be such a wife you need the qualification and the labor. This is especially clear in this country. Not only in this country today, but in every country on this globe all the families know this. The wives have to feed the children properly and have to teach their children that they may gain an education. A church is a family and the elders are actually the mothers. They should cook and they should also educate.

This is why I say strongly that we need a change in our system. Our present practice is mainly to give a message. A message at the most could only stir you up, affording you some inspiration. Such a meeting is not an educational matter. To carry out some educational teaching we need something like a lesson book. Fifty-two weeks a year, every week, we need at least one or two lessons, consecutively, in a good sequence.

To educate children is a difficult job. School buildings must be built, schools must be set up, teachers must be trained, faculty members have to be organized, and classes have to be set up. So many things have to be done just for passing on the proper knowledge of the human culture to our children for their education. Also the mother has to coordinate with the school, knowing how to send the children to the school, what grade they will be in, and how to take care of their lesson books, charging them in homework and so forth.

This is a good illustration, but such a church as a family I have not yet seen. The elders still are doing just a kind of routine work according to the traditional system of Christianity, that is, to gather people together, sing a hymn, have some prayers, and give them a message. This is easy to do, but to take care of the meeting, as a housewife taking care of the children in cooking and in education, the elders have to labor. It is no wonder that Paul says that overseers must be apt to teach and the elders have to labor in word and teaching.

This is my heavy burden. All the elders have to change their mentality, to have a real turn from the way that we are taking today. We must turn our attention to the new way, that is, number one, to cook, and number two, to teach. Just as a housewife, you have to cook with adequate time the proper, nourishing, tasty, and inexpensive food for your family. Also you have to teach. Even though you send your children to schools for education, still at home you need to do the home teaching. If the mothers could not do the work of teaching at home, the children would have a hard time going on in their education. Today in every local church, the elders and the leading ones, including the sisters, should practice this. They should continually cook proper meals for all the saints, and they should always be apt to teach. To do this you need to labor much.

Among the Protestant denominations, the Southern Baptists have the biggest membership. They depend mainly upon their Sunday schools. Though their lesson books are not so deep or so rich, they are very practical. Their Sunday school lessons were not prepared or written in a light way. To write anything in a general way is easy. To write lesson books is not so easy. You must collect all the extracts on a certain topic and then organize them in a very economical way. You cannot write too many pages, nor can you list too many points, yet you must cover all the crucial points of a certain subject. Nearly all of us have an education, yet after graduating from college, who can compose one lesson book? Let those who have learned mathematics try to write a lesson book on mathematics. It is not easy.

This illustrates that to teach the saints to be proper teachers is not easy. You may know something, but to teach it is not easy. We need to practice. The Southern Baptists appreciate their Sunday school lessons. Many would not miss their lessons because of the benefit they may receive. This is one reason the Southern Baptists have such a large membership. They emphasize three things. Number one, they preach the gospel. Number two, they hold revivals, and number three, they teach Sunday school using their lesson books. This is not to say that we are to follow them or to imitate them. But there is a principle here: if we depend upon big speakers or good teachers to speak to us every week, or if we depend upon eloquent speakers to stir us up periodically, that will not work.

I would like to share a strong testimony of something which occurred recently in Taipei. During October, 1984, while visiting there, I did my best to help them change their way. I encouraged them to turn their attention from the big meetings to the small home meetings. Right away they took my word and set up 399 small group gatherings totaling approximately 4,000 saints. Now, about eleven months later, a phone call has come from Taipei. A leading one told me that last weekend 1,104 people were baptized. He stressed that there was no large gospel-preaching meeting, nor any splendid activity. These 1,104 people were brought in by these small meetings and individuals. From January, 1985, until now, they have also baptized four to five hundred college, high school, or junior high students. In addition to this, the church in Taipei has sent out in July twenty gospel teams formed through the small meetings to the nearby small cities and towns to preach. With this kind of move they baptized over 800 people. All totaled, the church in Taipei baptized over 2,500 people this year. This was not by big evangelists holding big gospel campaigns, but by small meetings. If every small group would bring in one new person per week, there would be 400 new ones weekly. At the end of one month there would be 1,600 people. It is no wonder 1,100 people were baptized last week. This is the reaping of their labor for the previous months. The total seems quite large, yet with 400 small groups, this averages to less than three new ones per group per month. If every group brought in three, the total number would be 1,200.

To practice such a church life the elders, leading ones, sisters, and brothers are always busy. Just to take care of the baptisms, there is the need to do a lot of work. In Taipei, hall one, besides the general meetings, they have small training groups. The newly baptized ones are taught certain lessons for approximately seven weeks. I believe that all the new ones should receive some type of training right away.

As we can see there is the need for somebody to carry out some specific kind of work. In Taipei, due to these 400 small meetings being active, all of the saints are busy. The entire church is stirred up, charged with something to do. Thus far I have only received confirming reports that these small group meetings do work. Now I am waiting to hear how they labor in the Word and labor in teaching.

In the home the mother should cook and teach. This is on her side. On the children's side, they have to eat properly and must learn to study properly. I believe as long as you have a good, diligent mother doing the proper cooking and teaching, most of the children will cooperate with her.

LABORING IN THE WORD AND TEACHING

We have printed thousands of pages of the truth and most of you have bought these pages and put them on your shelves. We all know the terms and the subject areas, but we just do not know how to present them, how to teach them to people. We can all add and subtract, yet we do not know how to teach. Now we must endeavor. First, the leading ones must rise up to become educated, equipped, and prepared by laboring in the Word and laboring in teaching. They then must bring the saints into these two experiences.

I would encourage all the saints in the Lord's recovery to rise up to diligently seek after the truth. We do have the groceries. This means that we have a lot of printed pages, a lot of messages. Regardless of how busy each of you are every day, I still believe that you could spare thirty minutes every day. You could spare ten minutes in the morning. Suppose you normally rise up by six in the morning. Could you not rise up ten minutes earlier? Surely you could. And you could spare ten minutes at lunch time. Spend ten minutes to get into the Word. Put a life-study message in your pocket and wherever you are, if you have the time, read a few pages. The life-study messages are not to replace your Bible. Rather the contents of the life-studies are all based upon the verses from the Bible. Then in the evening before bedtime it is so easy for everybody among us to spare fifteen minutes. Consider how much you have wasted your time in the past. Brothers and sisters, consider how much time you spend on the phone rather than on the Bible or the life-study messages. We always take an excuse saying, "I do not have the time," but you do have time to spend ten minutes looking at the newspaper. Would you please, for your education, for your edification, for your growth in the Lord's life, for the Lord's interests, and for His recovery, redeem your time from all those wastes? Do not spend that much time on the newspapers. Do not spend that much time on the phone. As long as you can answer what they want, do not induce them to talk more. Do everything to save some time. I believe that it would be easy for everyone among us to spare thirty minutes a day.

In addition to the life-study messages, you have the Bible, especially the Recovery Version with the notes. Nearly all the hard points have been explained in the notes. The notes will render you much life supply. If you open a life-study to any line, you will get the benefit, but I would rather propose to you that you read the life-study consecutively. Pick a message and begin to read and consider the verses quoted on the first page. At the most this will take four minutes. Gradually, bit by bit, you will get yourself properly educated in the truths.

First Timothy 2:4 tells us that God desires everyone to be saved. In addition to this, God desires that every saved one have the full knowledge of the truth. But it bothers me that we are not like this. In the past twelve years, as a farmer I have grown a lot of groceries for all of you, and thank the Lord that you have bought them and stored them. However, the only sad thing is that you do not cook them much and you do not eat them much. This is not proper. We have the groceries, but we do not have sufficient cooking and we do not have enough eating. All the groceries are lying there as a waste.

Learn to handle the word of Christ, which is the word of life. First, we have to let the word of Christ, the living Person, dwell in us. Then we speak by teaching. Ephesians 5:19 says, "Speaking to one another in psalms and hymns and spiritual songs," but Colossians 3:16 says, "Teaching and admonishing one another in psalms, hymns, and spiritual songs." Speaking is somewhat liberal, but teaching is with regulations. We all have to pick up the living word of the living Lord and then teach one another. Learn this. This is a word not only to the leaders, the elders, but to all the saints. Let the word of Christ dwell in you, teaching in all wisdom. It is difficult for the Bible students to determine whether the phrase "in all wisdom" qualifies "let the word...dwell in you" or qualifies "teaching." According to our punctuation it qualifies teaching: "In all wisdom teaching." In order to teach in all wisdom, you must first learn the Word in all wisdom. If you do not study the Bible with all wisdom, how could you teach it with all wisdom? In John 6:63 the Lord says, "The words which I have spoken unto you are spirit and are life." Whatever we teach, whatever we speak, should be words of life.

The elders should be apt to teach and should labor in word and in teaching (1 Tim. 3:2; 5:17). All these words should be the healthy words (1 Tim. 6:3; 2 Tim. 1:13), and the teaching should be according to godliness (1 Tim. 6:3). In 1 Timothy godliness simply means God manifested in the flesh (3:16). This means that you have to practice the principle of incarnation. When you speak, when you teach the healthy words of the Lord Jesus, you must exercise yourself to such an extent that people can see God manifested in you. This is to teach, to speak, according to godliness. This requires much learning and much practice.

We should not be that ignorant, remaining in the darkness of today's Christianity. Today there is just darkness, but the light is shining here in the Lord's recovery. We should get into the light so that we could be enlightened, rescued, and delivered from our ignorance. I surely look to the Lord that you would take this word and have a turn to practice what the Lord is doing today.

CHAPTER SEVEN

SPEAKING THE LIVING AND RICH WORD FOR FOUR THINGS

Scripture Reading: Acts 4:31; 8:4; 6:7; 12:24; 19:20; 1 Cor. 1:18; 12:8; 2 Tim. 4:2; 2 Thes. 3:1; Col. 4:3

In this message my burden is just to exhort you to learn to speak the living and rich word of God. If you read through the verses listed above you could see that each verse speaks about the word of God. Each one bears a crucial point. When you put all the points together, you could see that the spoken word is something living. It is not only living, but also rich. What we are charged to speak is the living and rich word of God. We have to learn how to speak the living and rich word of God.

SPEAKING WITH PRAYER, THE SPIRIT, AND BOLDNESS

When we speak the word of God, we have to speak it with boldness. In Acts 4:31 boldness is used for the speaking of the word of God. This boldness is very much related to the Spirit, and the Spirit is related to prayer. This one verse is comprised of these three things. While they were beseeching, that is, while they were asking, petitioning, or praying to God, they were filled economically, outwardly, with the Spirit of power. Through their prayer they experienced the Spirit. With the Spirit they spoke the word of God with boldness. You can see that the speaking of God's word here is related to three things: prayer, the Spirit, and boldness. You could not have boldness without the Spirit, and you could not experience the Spirit without praying. Prayer brings us the Spirit, and the Spirit is the boldness. It is not only that the Spirit gives us boldness, but the Spirit Himself is the boldness. Sometimes we are timid because we are short of the Spirit. Because we are short of the Spirit, we do not have the boldness. Boldness always comes from the Spirit, and the Spirit comes from our prayer. These three things, prayer, the Spirit, and boldness, are all wrapped up with our speaking. We have to learn to pray that we may get the Spirit. Then we will have the boldness to speak the word of God.

THE PROPER AND ADEQUATE SPEAKING

In this series of messages we have been stressing one thing: that we should always be speaking. We have made it quite clear that this speaking is a divine speaking which is for the meetings. The Christian meetings are for a purpose, and this purpose could not be carried out without speaking. If there is little speaking, then little of the meeting's purpose is accomplished. This purpose could only be carried out by the saints' proper and adequate speaking. I am concerned that you have not been adequately impressed and even more concerned that you may not be practicing this speaking.

In Acts 1:8 the word witness implies a great deal. The Lord Jesus said, "But you shall receive power when the Holy Spirit has come upon you, and you shall be My witnesses." A witness is a speaking one. We are chosen and appointed, even assigned to be His speaking ones. We all have to speak Him, speak for Him, and speak forth Him. This is our duty.

Revelation 12:11 says that the brothers overcome the accuser by three things. One of these is the word of their testimony. The word of our testimony is a weapon to defeat our enemy, the accuser. Therefore, we should not be silent, but open up our mouth to speak. We must speak throughout the day. All the time we have to be learning how to speak, how to be a genuine, constant, and instant speaker. You should speak the Lord's word continually. This is our daily duty. We were chosen, regenerated, appointed, and even assigned with this commission. It is good to sing, "This is my story, this is my song, speaking my Savior, all the day long." Learn to speak the living and rich word.

GAINING A DEPOSIT OF THE LIVING AND RICH WORD

If you are going to speak the living and rich word, you should not trust in some kind of inspiration. Suppose you have never learned English, yet you trust in spiritual inspiration to enable you to speak it. I assure you, you could wait until the Lord comes back, and you would still not be speaking English. To learn English you first have to learn the alphabet, then the words, then sentences. You have to study English for many years before you are able to speak it in a living and rich way. In the same way we could not have the living and rich word from the Bible just by inspiration. In the past you may have had the desire to speak something from the Bible, yet you felt that you were short of utterance, short of words. You did not have the living and rich word.

Paul's main thought in 1 Corinthians 12:8-11 is that the Spirit is distributing the word of wisdom and the word of knowledge to the saints while they are in the meetings. If you do not read the Bible and therefore lack a rich deposit of the divine Word, you will come to the meeting empty. Then, even if the inspiration comes, you will not have the deposit you need. If you are going to serve people with a rich feast, you first need to get the groceries. If you do not have the groceries, how could you cook a rich meal? It is impossible. We all have to spend adequate time to pick up the Lord's word from the Bible.

THE HOLY WORD AND THE HOLY SPIRIT

We have to thank the Lord that on this earth, two great gifts have been given to humankind and to God's chosen people. One of these is the Word, the Bible. In this universe and on this earth, there is such a book which is called "the Book," Bible is a Latin word that means "the Book." This is "the Book," the unique book. If today there were no Bible, the earth would be full of darkness. The Bible is one of the greatest gifts of the Lord to mankind.

Our God has also given us another gift, the Holy Spirit. The Lord Jesus as the very God went through the wonderful processes of incarnation, human living, the all-inclusive death, resurrection, and ascension. Through all these wonderful, excellent processes He eventually did two things. First, He breathed the Spirit of life into His disciples on the day of His resurrection. Then He took another step to pour out the Spirit upon His disciples in His ascension. In His resurrection He breathed the Spirit into us, and in His ascension He poured the Spirit upon us. In that way He baptized all of us into one Body. We have the Bible, the Holy Scriptures, and the Spirit, the Holy Spirit. These are the two greatest gifts which we have today.

However, we always neglect these two gifts. We may have the Bible on our shelf or even in our pocket, but it has never gotten into us as it should have. In addition, many times we grieve the Holy Spirit. Ephesians 4:30 says, "And do not grieve the Holy Spirit of God, in whom you were sealed unto the day of redemption." The Greek word "unto" implies "with a goal to reach." This means that the sealing is not once for all, but continuing, still going on. We are still under this sealing all the day long. The Spirit is sealing us until we reach the goal of the redemption of our body. However, the real situation is that most of the time we care neither for the Holy Spirit nor for the holy Word. Mainly we just care for ourselves. As Christians we have been saved by the Lord, and we have been graced by Him. Today we are seeking after Him and we love Him, yet we mostly care for ourselves, not for the holy Word or for the Holy Spirit. We need a turn to care for these two gifts. We have to enjoy these two gifts hour after hour, day by day.

We have to pick up the word from the Bible until we have a rich deposit. Then when we come to the meeting with such a deposit, at any time we can write a check for a hundred dollars, a thousand dollars, or even a million dollars. When you come to the meeting with a deposit of the living and rich word, surely the Spirit will distribute to you the deep word of wisdom and the rich word of knowledge. The way to keep such a deposit is by laboring on the Word of God. Just as we have no reason for not eating the physical food, regardless of how busy we may be, we have no reason for not taking the spiritual food. Christians today are so weak, so poor, and so low just because of the spiritual famine. They do not eat the spiritual food. They do not pick up the Word regularly. Even among us I still feel that there is such a famine. If you mean business with the Lord for His recovery, and if you do love Him, you have to love His Word. The Lord Jesus said clearly, "If anyone loves Me, he will keep My word" (John 14:23). We must take His Word daily. Learn to pick up the Word and gain a deposit. Then when you come to the meeting, it will be easy to receive some distribution from the Spirit, either the word of wisdom or the word of knowledge. In this way you will speak by the Spirit. For this you must have a praying spirit.

I have many experiences along this line, because I speak so much. Recently, before a meeting I felt I had no choice but to pray much. The inner feeling told me that a little prayer would not be adequate. That would be like going to the gas station to get your tires pumped up, but leaving before the tires are filled. You have to pray. Not only so, when you come to the meeting, you must come with a praying spirit. Then while you are speaking, you will speak with a praying spirit. While I am speaking, I am praying. I am trusting in the Lord. I believe that while I am speaking, He is one spirit with me. In this way you will spontaneously have the sensation, the assurance, that you are speaking the holy Word with the Holy Spirit. Then you will have the boldness. We need this kind of speaking. We need the saints today to speak the living and rich word by a praying spirit. Then through this praying spirit, you will surely participate in the Spirit, who is your boldness.

SPEAKING FOR FOUR PRACTICAL THINGS

Our speaking with prayer, the Spirit, and boldness is for four things. These four things are practical. The first is the preaching of the gospel. The second is the releasing of the truth. The ministering of life is third. The fourth is the recovering of the saints. We speak the holy Word for these four things: to preach the gospel, to release the truth, to minister life, and to recover the weaker ones.

Preaching the Gospel

Let us first consider the preaching of the gospel. On a recent weekend in Taipei 1,104 were baptized. These 1,104 newly baptized saints were all gained not through preaching, but through speaking. The 1,104 were brought in by just about ten percent of the church in Taipei. Only a little over three hundred practiced my instruction to speak the gospel. By speaking the gospel every day they brought in so many. This was by speaking, not by preaching. Learn to speak. We all have to pick up the habit of speaking.

As Christians, we are witnesses of Christ. We should speak Him, making this kind of speaking a habit. When you go to visit your aunt, forget about current events in the news and speak Christ to her. Build up such a habit. You have to believe that when you speak, the Holy Spirit always follows your speaking and honors your speaking, and people will be saved. Learn to speak the living word and learn to speak the rich word. When you speak to your aunt, do not say, "You have to believe in the Lord Jesus, otherwise you will go to hell." This kind of speaking will offend people. You have to learn to speak the rich Christ. Tell your aunt that five years ago you never knew how much the Lord Jesus was to you. Tell her by listing all the rich items of Christ. You may tell her, "Now I know Christ is God's power and wisdom to me. He is also my righteousness, my sanctification, and my redemption."

If you are going to speak such a rich word you have to study 1 Corinthians 1. Learn to pick up the riches in the Word. First Corinthians 1 also tells us that we are the called saints, that Christ is ours, which means Christ is our portion, and that we have been called by the faithful God into the fellowship, the enjoyment or the participation of this portion. Now for us to enjoy this portion, God gives us Christ as power and as wisdom that we may receive Him as our righteousness, our justification; as our sanctification, our holiness; and also as our redemption. You have to pick up all these points from this one chapter.

Actually, today this is easy for you to do because you have the Recovery Version. All these rich items of Christ in

1 Corinthians 1 are pointed out in the footnotes. If you say you do not understand some of these points then you can go to the life-study messages. Some messages purposely explain what it means for Christ to be our sanctification, and why He is firstly our righteousness, then secondly our sanctification, and lastly our redemption. The life-study messages explain these points clearly. For this reason I strongly recommend the life-studies and the Recovery Version with the footnotes. From these two sources you can find the answers to all your questions and you can receive the living and rich word.

Human beings are always interested in knowing new things. In this top Christian country, the ears of the people are filled with going to heaven and going to hell. They do not like to hear any more of this. To them you need to speak something concerning the all-inclusive Christ. Pick up some rich word and speak to your relatives. Do not preach, just speak. To preach you may need to study at a seminary, but to speak you just need to pick up the habit. Learn to speak by speaking. Do not dream of a shortcut way saying, "I will fast for three weeks and then a great revival will come." Sixty years ago I studied about revivals and since then I have been watching. Honestly, within these past sixty years I have not seen or heard of one prevailing revival anywhere. God does not take the revival way. God just plants small potatoes like you and me. Then we all speak. If every Christian in this country would speak Christ, this would turn the American continent around. If you had a hundred great evangelists, I do not think you could accomplish this. We all must learn to speak. Do you not believe that through speaking Christ daily for one year someone would be saved? If we would speak, the number of saints would surely double. The doubling of our number is assured by our habitual speaking of the gospel. Just practice speaking; whether they believe or not is up to them.

Releasing the Truth

We must speak not only the gospel, but we must also speak the truth, the divine realities in the Bible. To speak the truth, you have to know the truth. There are many truths in the Bible. The Trinity is probably the greatest truth. Nearly all Christians know that our God is triune, the Father, the Son, and the Spirit, yet that is all they know. When asked to speak more concerning this they have little to say. We all must learn to speak something deeper. You can tell people that to be baptized is to be baptized into the Father, the Son, and the Spirit (Matt. 28:19). Then they will enjoy the grace of Christ the Son and the love of God the Father and will have a share in the fellowship of the Holy Spirit. They will enjoy the riches of the Trinity. You may think it would be hard to pick up all these points, but I do not think so. It all depends upon you. If you have the heart and the desire, you can surely do it, especially if you go to the Recovery Version, where there is a long note on 2 Corinthians 13:14. This note gives a long list of the references concerning the divine Trinity, from Genesis to Revelation. Furthermore, 1 Peter 1:2 says, "According to the foreknowledge of God the Father, in sanctification of the Spirit, unto obedience and sprinkling of the blood of Jesus Christ...." This is the very enjoyment of the Triune God. Then Paul in Ephesians 3 said that he bowed his knees to the Father, that He would strengthen us by the Spirit that Christ may make His home in our hearts. Again you can see the Triune God. There are many verses like this, including John 14:17-20. These are the rich words. Learn to pick them up and to speak them. Twelve years ago you might have had a lot of excuses not to speak the rich word, but not today. This is because I have put a lot of rich groceries in your pantry or at least at the book counter where you can get them. Now you can get all the riches.

In our training on the book of Acts we stressed the matter of dispensational transfer. I am concerned that many of us may have missed this crucial point. We need to spend a lot of time on all the notes that deal with this transfer in the book of Acts. I believe that in just half a day you will pick up a strong point concerning the dispensational transfer found in the book of Acts. I hope that you would spend some time to pick up the riches of the Word. Then when you speak, you would speak not only livingly, but also richly.

I am thankful to the Lord that many have been attending

the ministry meetings for over twelve years. I do believe the reason you have kept attending is because I do not render you some cheap things, some dead things, speaking things in a poor way. Whatever I have delivered to you has been at least somewhat living and rich. The livingness and the richness of this ministry attracts you. We all have to learn to speak not only the living word, but also the rich word. Then our speaking of the rich word will be the release of the truth. There are so many truths in the Bible. For example, the book of Galatians is full of riches: "But when it pleased God...to reveal His Son in me" (1:15-16); "For I through law have died to law that I might live to God" (2:19); "I have been crucified with Christ, and it is no longer I who live, but Christ lives in me" (2:20); "until Christ is formed in you" (4:19); "For neither is circumcision anything nor uncircumcision, but a new creation" (6:15). With the Recovery Version and the life-studies, it is so easy to pick up all these riches. It would be a pity if you have been with us for over five years, yet are still not so full of the riches of the holy Word. You are in a rich family with many riches. On your left side there are riches. On your right side there are riches. In back of you, in front of you, above and below you, there are many riches, but all the riches are not in you. We all need to realize the situation and pick up the riches of the holy Word that we may speak to people the living and rich word.

Ministering Life

Our speaking with prayer, the Spirit, and boldness is also for the ministering of life. Life is conveyed in the holy Word. The Bible is the word of life. Whatever we speak as the living, rich word of God is the word of life. We speak the word, but within the word is life. Therefore, in our speaking we spontaneously minister life to others. However, due to our shortage in the Word of God, when we try to help others, we just do not have the utterance to say anything. The most we could say might be, "You have to love the Lord, and realize that the Lord loves you and is trustworthy." Instead we need to minister something new, something of our own experience, something that we have discovered, something that we have gone through. By doing this we will spontaneously minister life to others. We need the proper speaking of the living, rich word so that we can minister life to others.

If you would do these three things—preach the gospel, release the truth, and minister life to others by speaking the living, rich word—then when you come to a big meeting or a small meeting you will be so rich. You will have the habit to speak, and you will have a lot to speak about, even to speak with. You would have a lot. I would have a lot; each one of us would have a lot. In this way the meeting would never be poor, low, dead, or cold. It would always be uplifted, enriched, and quite living. This is the way to have the church life built in the small meetings.

Recovering the Weaker Ones

The rich speaking also helps us to recover the weaker ones. In the church there are always a number of weaker ones. They need your support; they need your comfort; they need your help through the rich word by the Spirit.

In conclusion, if we really mean business with the Lord in His recovery, we all have to rise up. Do not take the shortcut way. Prepare yourself with a lot of endurance, a lot of divine patience to take this way for at least three or four years. Go to the small meetings, always spend your time to get into the holy Word, pray properly, and learn to speak habitually the things concerning Christ. Speak the divine riches firstly to build yourself up. Then you come to the meeting to practice this habit of speaking. Do not say, "I do not feel that I have the burden to speak anything in the meeting. I am not led; I have no inspiration." Forget about this traditional way. Learn to enter into the Word and pray about it, and then practice speaking according to the deposit in you. Then when you come to the meeting, whether or not you have the feeling that you are inspired or led, you will just speak. First your speaking will build up yourself, and then it will spontaneously build up others. Thus, the meetings will be built up. This is the way for the church life.

About the Author

Witness Lee was born in 1905 in northern China and raised in a Christian family. At age 19 he was fully captured for Christ and immediately consecrated himself to preach the gospel for the rest of his life. Early in his service, he met Watchman Nee, a renowned preacher, teacher, and writer. Witness Lee labored together with Watchman Nee under his direction. In 1934 Watchman Nee entrusted Witness Lee with the responsibility for his publication operation, called the Shanghai Gospel Bookroom.

Prior to the Communist takeover in 1949, Witness Lee was sent by Watchman Nee and his other co-workers to Taiwan to ensure that the things delivered to them by the Lord would not be lost. Watchman Nee instructed Witness Lee to continue the former's publishing operation abroad as the Taiwan Gospel Bookroom, which has been publicly recognized as the publisher of Watchman Nee's works outside China. Witness Lee's work in Taiwan manifested the Lord's abundant blessing. From a mere 350 believers, newly fled from the mainland, the churches in Taiwan grew to 20,000 in five years.

In 1962 Witness Lee felt led of the Lord to come to the United States, settling in California. During his 35 years of service in the U.S., he ministered in weekly meetings and weekend conferences, delivering several thousand spoken messages. Much of his speaking has since been published as over 400 titles. Many of these have been translated into over fourteen languages. He gave his last public conference in February 1997 at the age of 91.

He leaves behind a prolific presentation of the truth in the Bible. His major work, *Life-study of the Bible,* comprises over 25,000 pages of commentary on every book of the Bible from the perspective of the believers' enjoyment and experience of God's divine life in Christ through the Holy Spirit. Witness Lee was the chief editor of a new translation of the New Testament into Chinese called the Recovery Version and directed the translation of the same into English. The Recovery Version also appears in a number of other languages. He provided an extensive body of footnotes, outlines, and spiritual cross references. A radio broadcast of his messages can be heard on Christian radio stations in the United States. In 1965 Witness Lee founded Living Stream Ministry, a non-profit corporation, located in Anaheim, California, which officially presents his and Watchman Nee's ministry.

Witness Lee's ministry emphasizes the experience of Christ as life and the practical oneness of the believers as the Body of Christ. Stressing the importance of attending to both these matters, he led the churches under his care to grow in Christian life and function. He was unbending in his conviction that God's goal is not narrow sectarianism but the Body of Christ. In time, believers began to meet simply as the church in their localities in response to this conviction. In recent years a number of new churches have been raised up in Russia and in many eastern European countries.

Other Books Published By
Living Stream Ministry

Titles by Witness Lee:

Abraham—Called by God	0-7363-0359-6
The Experience of Life	0-87083-417-7
The Knowledge of Life	0-87083-419-3
The Tree of Life	0-87083-300-6
The Economy of God	0-87083-415-0
The Divine Economy	0-87083-268-9
God's New Testament Economy	0-87083-199-2
The World Situation and God's Move	0-87083-092-9
Christ vs. Religion	0-87083-010-4
The All-inclusive Christ	0-87083-020-1
Gospel Outlines	0-87083-039-2
Character	0-87083-322-7
The Secret of Experiencing Christ	0-87083-227-1
The Life and Way for the Practice of the Church Life	0-87083-785-0
The Basic Revelation in the Holy Scriptures	0-87083-105-4
The Crucial Revelation of Life in the Scriptures	0-87083-372-3
The Spirit with Our Spirit	0-87083-798-2
Christ as the Reality	0-87083-047-3
The Central Line of the Divine Revelation	0-87083-960-8
The Full Knowledge of the Word of God	0-87083-289-1
Watchman Nee—A Seer of the Divine Revelation ...	0-87083-625-0

Titles by Watchman Nee:

How to Study the Bible	0-7363-0407-X
God's Overcomers	0-7363-0433-9
The New Covenant	0-7363-0088-0
The Spiritual Man 3 volumes	0-7363-0269-7
Authority and Submission	0-7363-0185-2
The Overcoming Life	1-57593-817-0
The Glorious Church	0-87083-745-1
The Prayer Ministry of the Church	0-87083-860-1
The Breaking of the Outer Man and the Release ...	1-57593-955-X
The Mystery of Christ	1-57593-954-1
The God of Abraham, Isaac, and Jacob	0-87083-932-2
The Song of Songs	0-87083-872-5
The Gospel of God 2 volumes	1-57593-953-3
The Normal Christian Church Life	0-87083-027-9
The Character of the Lord's Worker	1-57593-322-5
The Normal Christian Faith	0-87083-748-6
Watchman Nee's Testimony	0-87083-051-1